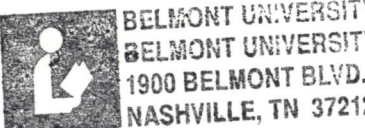

Papers of the Center for Research and Documentation
on World Language Problems

4

Language Status in the Post-Cold-War Era

Edited by
Kurt E. Müller

Series Editor
Humphrey Tonkin

UNIVERSITY
PRESS OF
AMERICA

Lanham • New York • London

Center for Research and
Documentation on World
Language Problems
Rotterdam, Netherlands, and
University of Hartford, USA

Copyright © 1996 by
University Press of America,® Inc.
4720 Boston Way
Lanham, Maryland 20706

3 Henrietta Street
London, WC2E 8LU England

All rights reserved
Printed in the United States of America
British Cataloging in Publication Information Available

Co-published by arrangement with the Center for Research and Documentation on World Language Problems, University of Hartford, West Hartford, CT. 06117, and Nieuwe Binnenweg 176,3015-BJ, Rotterdam, Netherlands

The views expressed by the author(s) of this publication do not necessarily represent the opinions of the Center for Research and Documentation on World Language Problems.

Library of Congress Cataloging-in-Publication Data

Language status in the post-Cold-War era / edited by Kurt E. Müller.
p.   cm. --(Papers of the Center for Research and Documentation on World Language Problems ;4)
"Based on papers delivered at various conferences...whose themes were 'Language and international education : a review of priorities' and "Language and international communication in the post-Cold-War era"--CIP pref.
Includes bibliographical references.
1. Language and languages--Political aspects. 2. Communication, International. 3. Language and languages--Study and teaching. 4. Multicultural education. 5. World politics--1989- I. Müller, Kurt E. II. Series.
P119.3.L367   1996   400--dc20   96-10297 CIP

ISBN 0-7618-0299-1 (cloth: alk. ppr.)

⊖™ The paper used in this publication meets the minimum requirements of American National Standard for information Sciences—Permanence of Paper for Printed Library Materials, ANSI Z39.48—1984

206933
BELMONT UNIVERSITY LIBRARY

To Liz

*an ever-present cocelebrant of life
and supporter in time of need*

Contents

Preface vii

Antaŭparolo xi

An Introduction to Language and International
    Communication in the Post-Cold-War Era
  Françoise Cestac 1

Ethnolinguistic Democracy:
    Varieties, Degrees, and Limits
  Joshua A. Fishman 7

Is Linguistic Evolution in the United Nations
    a Consequence of Recent Political Evolution?
  Jean Gazarian 23

Changes in the Pattern of Language
    Use in the United Nations
  Stephen B. Pearl 29

The Role of Russian in the Post-Cold-War Era
  Alexandre K. Titov 43

The Perestroika of the Russian Language:
    From Marx to Marketing
  Lynn Visson 49

The Contribution of Language Planning and
    Language Policy to the Reconciliation of Unity
    and Diversity in the Post-Cold-War Era
  Timothy Reagan 59

Language Study and Global Education: Approaches
  to Development of Language and Communication
  for Bridge-Building in the Post-Cold-War Era
  Helene Zimmer-Loew 67

Global Awareness and Language Learning
  Margareta Bowen 73

Interpreter Training:
  The Stepchild of Language Teaching
  Lynn Visson 91

Linguistic Pluralism for Internationalization: The Case for Non-
  Traditional Approaches to Language Study for U.S. Schools
  Timothy Reagan and Karen Case 97

Integrating Language and Global Education
  Ronald J. Glossop 109

From Attitudes toward the Foreign to the Development
  of Children's International Literacy
  Kurt E. Müller 117

A Brief Response to Kurt Müller
  Ronald J. Glossop 137

Language Equality at the United Nations: An Achievable Dream
  Humphrey Tonkin 141

About the Contributors 149

Preface

This is the fourth volume in the series of Papers of the Center for Research and Documentation on World Language Problems. As with its predecessors, it is based on papers delivered at various conferences cosponsored by the Center and the Office of Conference Services of the United Nations. This collection originates with conferences whose themes were "Language and International Education: A Review of Priorities" and "Language and International Communication in the Post-Cold-War Era." As readers will see from the following chapters, language status and language education are intertwined, if not related.

Françoise Cestac introduces our volume with a range of diplomatic concerns that set the stage for language support to these issues. The UN secretary general's report to the Security Council, *An Agenda for Peace*, with its emphasis on preventive diplomacy, peacemaking, peacekeeping, and peacebuilding, becomes the background for the concerns of language professionals, from interpreters and translators to language teachers to sociolinguists.

Relations between language and politics can be explored from many perspectives. Although the chapters that follow are not restricted to any one perspective, they share a tone of mutual respect for multiple cultures and their expression through a diversity of languages, a level of regard not always present at international levels and more frequently absent within specific nations. Joshua Fishman points out such differentials in noting that "bilingual proficiency [is] typically ... asymmetrical and a reflection of power differentials, such that the situationally weaker party is far more often bilingual than the stronger." Fishman points as well to differences evident in the treatment of "small" languages at the international political level compared with the treatment minority languages may receive within nations.

Several contributors look at the evolution of language use in the United Nations. Jean Gazarian reviews the status of official languages and notes a trend toward the use of unofficial languages by speakers who provide their own interpretation into one of the official ones. Specifically with regard to the use of Russian, individual contributors look at the evolution in the use (or avoidance) of Russian at the United Nations, the role of Russian as a means of unification and dissemination of knowledge in the former Soviet Union, and Western influences on the development of Russian.

Stephen Pearl turns on its head the obvious logic behind the need for interpreters, using the very experience of the United Nations as evidence for a thesis (which I'll not divulge here) that should be read in the context of ethnolinguistic democracy set out for us by Joshua Fishman. In particular, the existence of official languages imposes constraints on those nations whose languages are not granted official status, perhaps less so in formal, diplomatic relations and more so in circumstances requiring technical expertise in the exchange of scientific and cultural information and the development of transnational policies dependent on subject matter expertise.

Alexandre Titov provides a perspective on the use of Russian as a lingua franca for the 130 nationalities that made up the former USSR. His insights will be appreciated as well by those whose interests have little to do with the Soviet Union and much to do with language in multicultural societies. His remarks about "Communist bosses who, through insufficient educational or cultural background treated languages without respect, not understanding the delicate nature of this most important feature of human experience and cultural tradition" inform those of us whose interests in language status may concern South Asia, Western Europe, North America, or any other part of the world.

Reactions to Russian rhetoric are informed by Lynn Visson's consideration of phrases used in the USSR during the Cold War whose subsurface meanings are clearly at odds with a "face value" reading of the elocutions she presents. In a manner that requires no specialist in Slavic languages to appreciate, Visson places recent Western lexical borrowing in a much longer historical context of Western influence on Russian language and culture.

Choice of language conveys a message as well as its content. This theme recurs in treatments by Stephen Pearl, Timothy Reagan, and Ronald Glossop and is somewhat below the surface in several other chapters. Reagan looks at language policy and language planning with a clear modus operandi of demonstrating respect for diversity. If language is a touchstone for both ethnic identity and political opposition, Reagan proposes that national-level language policy should follow the primary edict of medical treatment: *primum nihil nocere*—national language policies should not exacerbate the assimilation or recognition of various ethnic groups.

Helene Zimmer-Loew reports on initiatives undertaken by the Council for Cultural Cooperation of the Council of Europe. The Council's initiatives to produce a European identity are designed to simultaneously appreciate regional diversity and encourage multilingualism across Europe. The Council's approach looks at national institutions and deliberately exploits the traditional training of tradesmen and artisans, promoting multilingualism in vocational education, secondary and university education, and technology appropriate to life-long learning.

If language education and European identity both conserve national identities and develop pan-European perspectives, we should look to interrelations between language learning and world knowledge. In American education in particular, this connection is not a simple one and may even have been deliberately undermined. If so, it becomes less surprising that in such studies as the "Other Nations Other Peoples" project, undertaken by the Educational Testing Service (best known for its tests broadly used by colleges and universities in admissions processing), and the "Education and the World View" project undertaken by the Council on Learning, the original sponsor of *Change* (a magazine oriented toward North American higher education), those students with substantial exposure to other languages are not necessarily more aware of world developments than are students whose primary focus is in history or social sciences. Margareta Bowen shows us that knowledge of world affairs contributes to the ability to translate and interpret between languages but majoring in a language may not be sufficient to deal with the subject matter that arises in interpretation tasks. The technical tasks of translation have been deemphasized in language teaching as language pedagogy has tended to promote speaking proficiency over academic knowledge of the target language. But is something lost through this shift in emphasis? Lynn Visson finds a dearth of information on language professions such as interpreting and translating and materials to prepare for these careers and advocates attention to translating in developing a concern for accuracy of delivering a message across cultures. The very documents produced by professionals at the United Nations might well be used in support of language teaching.

Timothy Reagan and Karen Case look at foreign language education in the United States and declare it a failure on the basis of "brief and ineffective exposure to languages other than English." To make children more aware of language issues, they propose exposure in elementary and secondary schools to various language themes, such as the general nature of human languages, and exposure to various languages early in schooling. Their choice of language is not limited to the most frequently taught (worldwide) but includes African languages, sign language, and Esperanto.

Promotion of Esperanto as a means toward becoming more globally aware is the central theme of Ronald Glossop's chapter. He advocates Esperanto especially for an anglophone society inasmuch as he sees English as the only truly global, natural language at the moment. He makes the case that the very dominance of English as the first foreign language elsewhere contributes to the need for anglophone children to learn another language. If we are to promote global education, we cannot abide a situation in which anglophone children learn through their own experience of global education in their schools that they do not need to learn any other language to learn about the rest of the world.

In assembling these chapters, I have exercised an editorial prerogative in appending a "counterpaper," as it were, to provide a counterpoint to several suggestions occurring in these chapters. As I worked through several of the papers, I found I disagreed with a number of proposals, often less with their specifics than with the impact that could result if some of these suggestions are adopted. Since education in more than one language strikes me as essential, I cannot let stand unchallenged any curricular proposals inimical to expanding language instruction.

For its acceptance of this added paper, I am truly indebted to the Center for Research and Documentation on World Language Problems, particularly to Humphrey Tonkin, whose closing chapter returns us to some of our opening themes. For his forebearance in allowing delays in publication necessitated by my government service abroad in primitive circumstances, I am likewise grateful.

K.E.M.
Hamilton, New Jersey

Antaŭparolo

Jen la kvara volumo en la serio de referaĵoj de la Centro de Esploro kaj Dokumentado pri la Monda Lingvo-Problemo (CED). Same kiel la antaŭaj volumoj, ĝi baze konsistas el referaĵoj prezentitaj en la diversaj konferencoj kune aŭspiciataj de la CED kaj de la Oficejo de Konferencaj Servoj ĉe Unuiĝintaj Nacioj. La kolekto fontas el konferencoj, kies temoj estis "Lingvoj kaj internacia edukado: Rerigardo al la prioritatoj" kaj "Lingvoj kaj internacia komunikado en la periodo post la Malvarma Milito." Kiel la legantoj tuj vidos en la sekvaj ĉapitroj, demandoj pri lingva statuso kaj lingva edukado interligiĝas, aŭ eĉ parencas.

Françoise Cestac enkondukas nian volumon per prezento de diplomatiaj demandoj, kiuj pretigas la scenejon por lingva apogo. La raporto de la ĝenerala sekretario de UN al la Sekureca Konsilio, *Tagordo por paco*, kiu emfazas anticipan diplomation, pacfaradon, packonservadon, kaj packonstruadon, fariĝas fono por la zorgoj de lingvoprofesiuloj, ekde interpretistoj kaj tradukistoj ĝis lingvoinstruistoj kaj socilingvistoj.

Oni povas esplori lingvon kaj politikon el multaj vidpunktoj. Kvankam la ĉi-sekvaj ĉapitroj ne limiĝas al unu difinita aliro, ili ĉiuj montras tonon de reciproka respekto al la multeco de kulturoj kaj ilia esprimiĝo tra lingvodiverseco—nivelo de respekto, kiu ne ĉiam evidentas en internaciaj rondoj kaj kutime plene mankas ene de specifaj nacioj. Joshua Fishman aludas al tiaj diferencigoj atentigante, ke "dulingva kapablo [estas] kutime ... malsimetria, respegulante diferencojn de potenco, tiel, ke la rolanto kun pli malforta pozicio montriĝas dulingva multe pli ofte ol la pli forta." Fishman ankaŭ montras al diferencoj en traktado de "malgrandaj" lingvoj je la internacia politika nivelo kompare kun traktado, kiun ricevas minoritataj lingvoj ene de landoj.

Pluraj kontribuantoj ekzamenas la evoluon de lingvouzo en Unuiĝintaj Nacioj. Jean Gazarian trarigardas la statuson de oficialaj lingvoj kaj rimarkas ĉe parolantoj plioftiĝon de la praktiko utiligi neoficialajn lingvojn kaj liveri propran interpretadon en unu el la oficialaj. Specife ĉe la rusa lingvo, kontribuantoj esploras la evoluon en utiligo (aŭ evito) de tiu lingvo en Unuiĝintaj Nacioj, la rolon de la rusa kiel ilo por unuecigi kaj disvastigi informojn en la iama Sovetunio, kaj okcidentajn influojn sur la lingva evoluo de la rusa.

Stephen Pearl renversas la evidentan logikon malantaŭ la neceso havi interpretistojn, utiligante precize la sperton de Unuiĝintaj Nacioj kiel pruvon al tezo (kiun mi ne malkaŝos tie ĉi), kiun oni devus legi en la kunteksto de tiu etnolingva demokratio prezentita al ni de Joshua Fishman. Specife, la ekzisto de oficialaj lingvoj limigas tiujn naciojn, kies lingvoj ne ricevas oficialan statuson, ne tiom en formalaj, diplomatiaj rilatoj, kiom en cirkonstancoj, kiuj postulas teknikan kapablon en sciencaj kaj kulturaj interŝanĝoj, kaj en evoluigo de transnaciaj politikoj, kiuj fontas el faka scio.

Alexandre Titov liveras perspektivon pri la utiligo de la rusa kiel interlingvo inter la 130 naciecoj, kiuj konsistigis la iaman Sovetunion. Lian klarvidon agnoskos ankaŭ tiuj, kies interesoj malmulte rilatas al Sovetunio sed rekte ligiĝas al la rolo de lingvoj en multkulturaj socioj. Liaj rimarkoj pri "komunistaj ĉefoj, kiuj pro nesufiĉa eduka aŭ kultura scio traktis lingvojn sen respekto, ne komprenante la delikaton de tiu plej grava aspekto de la homa sperto kaj kultura tradicio," reeĥas al tiuj inter ni, kies interesoj pri lingva statuso eventuale rilatas al Suda Azio, Okcidenta Eŭropo, Nordameriko, aŭ kiu ajn alia mondoparto.

Reagoj al rusa retoriko ankaŭ pliprofundiĝas pro konsideroj pri frazeroj uzataj en Sovetunio dum la Malvarma Milito, kies subsurfacaj signifoj evidente kontraŭas surfacan interpreton de la koncernaj parolturnoj. Lynn Visson, aŭtoro de tiu referaĵo, lokigas, en maniero, kiu ne postulas apartan slavistikan scion, okcidentajn leksikajn pruntojn en pli longan historion de okcidentaj influoj sur la rusan lingvon kaj kulturon.

Ne nur enhavo, sed ankaŭ lingvoelekto, mesaĝas. Tiu temo aperas en la traktaĵoj de Stephen Pearl, Timothy Reagan kaj Ronald Glossop, kaj sidas iom subsurface en pluraj aliaj ĉapitroj. Reagan alrigardas lingvopolitikon kaj lingvoplanadon kun klara celo montri respekton al diverseco. Se la lingvo estas ilo por difini etnecon kaj politikan opozicion, Reagan proponas, ke nacinivela lingvopolitiko sekvu la unuavican principon de medicina kuraco: *primum nihil nocere*—nacia lingvopolitiko ne akrigu la asimiliĝon aŭ rekonon de la diversaj etnoj.

Helene Zimmer-Loew raportas pri iniciatoj de la Konsilio pri Kultura Kunlaboro de la Konsilio de Eŭropo. La iniciatoj de tiu Konsilio por krei eŭropan identecon celas samtempe valorigi regionan diversecon kaj instigi al plurlingvismo trans Eŭropo. La aliro de la Konsilio fokusiĝas al naciaj institucioj kaj intence ekspluatas la tradician trejnadon de metiistoj kaj manlaboristoj, per antaŭenigo de multlingvismo en metia edukado, meznivela kaj universitata edukado, kaj teknologio taŭga al daŭra lernado.

Se lingva edukado kaj eŭropa identeco samtempe konservas naciajn identecojn kaj evoluigas tuteŭropajn perspektivojn, ni rigardu al rilatoj inter lingvolernado kaj scio pri la mondo. Precipe en usona edukado, tiu ligo ne estas tiel simpla, kaj foje oni eĉ intence subfosis ĝin. Se tiel estas, ni malpli surpriziĝu, ke en studoj kiel la projekto "Aliaj Nacioj Aliaj Popoloj" de Educational Testing Service (plej bone konata pro siaj testoj vaste uzataj por enlasi studentojn en superan edukadon), kaj la projekto "Edukado kaj la Monda Vidpunkto" de Council on Learning, la unua apoganto de *Change* (revuo orientita al nordamerika supera edukado), tiuj studentoj kun signifa kontakto kun aliaj lingvoj ne nepre montriĝas pli konsciaj pri mondaj aferoj ol tiuj, kiuj ĉefe fokusiĝas al historio aŭ sociaj sciencoj. Margareta Bowen montras al ni, ke scio pri mondaj aferoj kontribuas al kapablo traduki kaj interpreti, kaj ke diplomiĝo pri difinita lingvo eble ne sufiĉos por trakti la sciomaterialon, kiu ekaperas en interpretaj taskoj. Teknikaj tradukaj taskoj lastatempe ricevas malpli da emfazo ĉar la lingvopedagogio emas plivalorigi parolan kapablon super akademian scion de la cellingvo. Sed ĉu pro tiu ŝovo de emfazo oni ion perdis? Lynn Visson rimarkas mankon de informoj pri la lingvaj profesioj (interpretado, tradukado ktp.) kaj de materialoj preparaj al tiuj karieroj. Ŝi rekomendas atenton al tradukado por kreskigi zorgon pri precizeco en liverado de mesaĝoj trans kulturoj. La dokumentojn produktitajn de profesiuloj ĉe Unuiĝintaj Nacioj oni povus uzi por subteni lingvoinstruadon.

Timothy Reagan kaj Karen Case ekzamenas fremdlingvan edukadon en Usono kaj deklaras ĝin malsukceso surbaze de "mallonga kaj senefika malfermiĝo al lingvoj aliaj ol la angla." Por igi infanojn pli konsciaj pri lingvaj demandoj, ili proponas utiligon de diversaj lingvaj temoj en elementaj kaj mezaj lernejoj, ekzemple la ĝenerala karaktero de homaj lingvoj, kaj lernado pri diversaj lingvoj frue en la edukado. La aŭtoroj ne limigas la lingvoelekton al la plej instruataj mondolingvoj, sed ili inkluzivas afrikajn lingvojn, gestolingvojn, kaj Esperanton.

Antaŭenigo de Esperanto kiel ilo por monda konsciiĝo formas la centran temon de la ĉapitro de Ronald Glossop. Li rekomendas Esperanton precipe por anglalingvaj socioj ĉar li rigardas la anglan la sola vere tutmonda natura lingvo en la nuna tempo. Li argumentas, ke precize pro superrego de la angla kiel la unua fremda lingvo ekster anglalingvaj landoj, nepras, ke anglalingvaj infanoj lernu alian lingvon. Se ni celas tergloban edukadon, ni ne povas akcepti situacion, en kiu anglalingvaj infanoj lernas per sia sperto de tergloba edukado en la propraj lernejoj, ke ne necesas lerni alian lingvon por scii pri la cetero de la mondo.

Redaktante tiujn ĉapitrojn, mi aplikis redaktoran prerogativon aldonante ian "kontraŭreferaĵon," por liveri alian vidpunkton reage al pluraj sugestoj, kiuj aperas en tiuj ĉi ĉapitroj. Dum mi tralaboris kelkajn referaĵojn, mi rimarkis, ke mi malkonsentas pri pluraj rekomendoj—ne tiom pro iliaj specifaĵoj kiom pro la probablaj rezultoj se aplikiĝus tiuj sugestoj. Ĉar mi opinias edukadon en pli ol unu lingvo esenca, mi ne povas lasi sen respondo studprogramajn proponojn kontraŭajn al plivastigo de lingvoinstruado.

Pro ties akcepto de tiu aldona referaĵo, mi multon ŝuldas al la Centro de Esploro kaj Dokumentado pri la Monda Lingvo-Problemo, kaj precipe al Humphrey Tonkin, kies ferma ĉapitro resendas nin al kelkaj niaj komencaj temoj. Pro lia indulgo pri prokrastoj kaŭzitaj de mia ŝtata servado eksterlande en primitivaj cirkonstancoj mi estas aparte danka.

K.E.M.
Hamilton, Novĵerzeo

An Introduction to Language and International Communication in the Post-Cold-War Era

Françoise Cestac

As simplistic as it may appear to say, since 1989 the world has witnessed and lived through radical political realignments which have continued to have a profound impact on established patterns of communication and language use. The break-up of the Soviet Union and the emergence of newly independent states have changed the role of Russian as the shared language of the former Soviet republics and have opened much of Central Asia to new linguistic influences. With the reappearance of the concept of Central Europe and the reunification of Germany, the international significance of the German language has grown. The push toward market economies has brought with it a redistribution of linguistic roles within Eastern and Central Europe. Indeed, a whole approach, linguistic as well as philosophical, to the interpretation and articulation of political, economic, and social problems, has, in part, forfeited its relevance. Meanwhile, a new linguistic landscape seems to be emerging as a result of disintegrative tendencies linked to the resurgence of pre-World War II nationalities, which have affected the ways in which people and political movements express their needs and frame their aspirations.

We at the United Nations concern ourselves with the reciprocal nature of the relationship between language and multiculturalism, and we respect its balance of unity and diversity. We know that as we contribute through language to the rich mosaic of multiculturalism that exists in the world, this multiculturalism will continue to be a source of enrichment for the Organization and will be a *force majeure* in achieving the goals of the United Nations.

We know that the wealth of countries lies in the diversity of their cultures and languages. However, differences of language, from country to country and within individual countries, have sometimes given rise to problems, from relatively mild issues of services and government notices to power struggles among competing groups. Despite notable progress in education and in the management of multilingualism within and between countries, apprehension and anxiety remain today in circumstances where multiple languages are used. The issue confronted not only by the United Nations, but also by governments, social planners, and ordinary citizens is how to balance unity and diversity, how to bring the benefits of political and economic participation to all without at the same time destroying the integrity of individual communities and cultures.

Similar topics have caught the attention of other fora. Recently, I was invited to participate in a seminar sponsored by the European Institute. The general theme was: "Multilingualism in Europe and the United States: A Communication Challenge for Transatlantic Relations and Global Business." I chose to speak about lessons from multilateral organizations in communication with international partners. In essence, I wanted to go beyond the two continents and share the experience gained through communication in and between other states and regions of the world.

We view improved communication in the post-Cold-War era as an essential component of our international activities. World events in recent years have empowered the United Nations to take all sorts of action it could never have attempted during the Cold War. The Cold War confronted the international community with a singular threat to security, but the old order has now been swept away in a torrent of change. In its place, we are confronted with new challenges in a widely varying array, and the present demands on the United Nations have no precedent. The world keeps changing, and new areas of concern take on significance, while old ones are being redefined in the context of the new world order. We see the question of humanitarian and emergency assistance taking on global proportions, while competition for resources in the economic and social fields grows, and we face the increasingly urgent question of peacekeeping.

In an environment like the United Nations, in which individuals who speak different languages and come from various cultures must interact daily, language is not just a conduit for communication. It also serves as the primary tool for creating and expressing cooperation. As an instrument for cooperation of the most timely relevance, we must consider the Agenda for Peace proposed by Mr. Boutros Boutros-Ghali, Secretary General of the United Nations.

In this regard, the Security Council and General Assembly are now considering a set of far-reaching proposals that reflect the world's renewed focus on the need to preserve—at the international level—world peace and security. In response to the first-ever summit meeting of the Security Council held in January 1992, a special report, entitled *An Agenda for Peace*, was prepared by the Secretary General. In the introduction to his report, the Secretary General stated that "the Summit represented an unprecedented recommitment, at the highest political level, to the purposes and principles of the Charter of the United Nations." He observed that "an opportunity had been regained to achieve the great objectives of the Charter: a United Nations capable of maintaining international peace and security, of securing justice and human rights and of promoting, in the words of the Charter, 'social progress and better standards of life in larger freedom'."

The Security Council specifically requested the Secretary General to report on the problems of preventive diplomacy, peacemaking, and peacekeeping. Bearing these in mind, the Secretary General identified another closely related concept: peacebuilding. He defined the aims of the United Nations in this context as follows:

> To seek to identify at the earliest possible stage situations that could produce conflict, and to try through *preventive diplomacy* to remove the sources of danger before violence results;
>
> Where conflict erupts, to engage in *peacemaking* aimed at resolving the issues that have led to conflict;
>
> Through *peace-keeping*, to work to preserve peace, however fragile, where fighting has been halted and to assist in implementing agreements achieved by the peacemakers;
>
> To stand ready to assist in *peace-building* in its differing contexts: rebuilding the institutions and infrastructures of nations torn by civil war and strife; and building bonds of peaceful mutual benefit among nations formerly at war;

And in the largest sense, to address the deepest causes of conflict: economic despair, social injustice and political oppression. (7–8, emphasis added)

To give an idea of how extensive the involvement of the United Nations is, since 1948, there have been 26 United Nations peacekeeping operations undertaken, and there are currently 13 underway around the world: Cambodia, Cyprus, El Salvador, Mozambique, Somalia, South Africa, and the former Yugoslavia, to name just a few. Still others are planned or are under discussion.

Clearly, in the pursuit of all these aims, communication in all its forms constitutes the indispensable component. Language as a means of facilitating communications has obvious importance at global conferences and meetings to target the aims of the Organization. In addition, it plays an important role in field operations and missions for preventive diplomacy, peacemaking, peacekeeping and peacebuilding. This may include: interpretation between negotiating parties, translation of messages between member states or other parties to negotiations, standardization of geographical names for maps or treaties, interpretation for training of operational staff, or translation of operations manuals for field personnel.

Having thus set the stage for our discussion, let us proceed to four main issues related to language and international communication in the post-Cold-War era:

- the *political perspective*, that is, the consequence of recent political realignments on established patterns of communication and language use
- the *linguistic perspective*, the redistribution of language patterns and the new linguistic landscape; what the implications of language are for national, regional, and international policy-making and planning
- *approaches to the development of language and internatonal communication* for bridge-building in the post-Cold-War era
- and *prospects and opportunities for enhancing communication* to build a new order; reconciling diversity and unity.

We have the good fortune of contributions from eminent persons, distinguished in their respective fields, who have accepted an invitation to discuss this fascinating and topical question. Their common denominator is experience—their testimony as witnesses to these radical changes as politicians, diplomats, economists, linguists, and academics.

As a final introductory comment, I wish to share a quote from Secretary General Boutros-Ghali's address to the General Assembly at the opening of the International Year of Indigenous People: "Unity through diversity is the only true and enduring unity." With that comment, the Secretary General called for a world-wide effort to protect human rights and preserve cultural authenticity. In our fora, the debates have traditionally been both serious and passionate. Partisans of cultural identities, of plurilingualism as a contribution to the universality of thought and communication, of monolingualism or of a single language offered to all will all express their views. In considering these contributions, we shall have learned a great deal in paving the way for a better understanding among people.

Work Cited

Boutros-Ghali, Boutros. *An Agenda for Peace: Preventive Diplomacy, Peacemaking, and Peace-keeping*. New York: United Nations, 1992. Report of the Secretary-General pursuant to the statement adopted by the Summit Meeting of the Security Council on 31 January 1992.

Ethnolinguistic Democracy: Varieties, Degrees, and Limits

Joshua A. Fishman

With the entry or re-entry of several Eastern European nationalities onto the stage of history as independent polities, the notion of ethnolinguistic democracy deserves to be pondered once again. This is so not only because their (re-)entry has implications for any consideration given this matter in previous times by such agencies as the European (Economic) Community, but because Eastern Europe in particular has long been the European heartland of the co-occurrence of languages, peoples, and religions and the elevation of this co-occurrence to the level of *Weltanschauung*. The centrality of language in ethnoreligious identity (and therefore in ethnomoral thought) has been a constant and long-recorded feature of eastern Mediterranean and Eastern European societies since our earliest records of them. The biblical Book of Esther, e.g., expresses this view both at the level of collectivities as well as at the level of individuals. When the King of the Medes and the Persians sent messages to the various provinces and peoples of his Empire, we are told that these messages were sent "into every province according to the writing thereof and to every people after their language" (Esth.1:22). The purpose of this diglossic arrangement—provinces having their interethnic written varieties but peoples having their own vernaculars—was distinctly a moral one, namely, "so that every man should bear rule in his own house." Presumably, these formulations are an early (perhaps the earliest) attempt to define a modus operandi in the realm of ethnolinguistic democracy: one based on the view that people and peoples are not treated honorably unless their own languages are utilized, particularly in speech and to some extent in writing as well.

In those far distant times, communications upwards to heads of states were not necessarily informed by concerns for reciprocity. The Good Book does not tell us of how Ahasuerus' subjects, or even those acting on behalf of an entire region of his empire, expected to address him, whether orally or in writing. However, from what we know from other sources about the usage of those times, it seems probable that such communications were conducted in the language of the central authorities of the empire. In our day and age, indeed, ever since the early 19th century, there have been some, particularly among the spokespersons for regional and immigrant collectivities, who have viewed the latter usage as undemocratic because, just as all people should be considered equal before the law, so all languages should somehow be considered equal as well. Of course, individuals, communities and polities are not all equal in power, but in a moral universe, these spokespersons have claimed, they should each be equally entitled to use their own language if they are so inclined, rather than necessarily expected to constantly show deference to some language associated with greater power. This, then, will be our first working definition of "complete ethnolinguistic democracy": the right of both parties in an interaction to use their own languages and to receive in their own languages in return, regardless of the power or size differentials that distinguish between them.

A Two-Dimensional Frame of Reference for Discussing Ethnocultural Democracy

Let us look more carefully at the two dimensions that are already implicit in our discussion thus far. On the one hand there is the consideration of the extent to which any party's (particularly the weaker party's) preferred language is operative in any interaction. If, through the provision of translators, one's own preferred language[1] can be operative both in encoding messages sent and in decoding messages received, then obviously the two parties to the interaction are totally equalized linguistically. Neither one has to accommodate to the other and neither one has to shoulder the burden of acquiring proficiency, whether active or passive, in the other's language (such bilingual proficiency typically being asymmetrical and a reflection of power differentials, such that the situationally weaker party is far more often bilingual than the stronger). At the opposite end of this dimension, past the end of the horizontal dimension in the table below, are those interactions where neither party is able to use its own language and where both have become bilingual but not in the native language of the other. Although complete reciprocity nominally also exists in the latter case, *both* parties being required to utilize a language not their own, this pattern really falls far short of complete ethnolinguistic equality. Unless the languages involved are International (Artificial) Auxiliary Languages (a case to which we will return later), they are inevitably (a) someone's mother tongue, (b) more accessible to some parties than to others, or (c) both of the above, and the aforementioned "someones" have a definite advantage in the ensuing interactions. Even when both parties freely set aside their mother tongues for the sake of a parsimonious interaction, such self-denial can be considered neither ethnolinguistically responsive nor ethno-identity supportive, no matter how commendable from the point of view of parsimony per se (as claimed, e.g., by Turi, 1992).

Mid-point on this first dimension (let us call it "degree of preferred language involvement"), between complete mother-tongue implementation and complete mother-tongue substitution, there are non-reciprocal arrangements whereby one party both sends and receives in its preferred tongue and the other either only receives or only sends. This is often a power-dominated interaction, as in our example from the Empire of the Medes and the Persians. However, this pattern is still more ethnolinguistically democratic than the even more restrictive ones just mentioned above, because the weaker party can at least send *or* receive messages in its own self-affirming code. When the latter option is removed, then we are left with a situation which is outside the limits of ethnolinguistic democracy.

The above three operative modes along the dimension of preferred language implementation by the weaker party intersect with another dimension which deals with the magnitude of scale pertaining to the interacting parties. This dimension is usually expressed in terms of political power and demographic numbers. At the top of this dimension there is the sovereign state, followed, in order of decreasing scale, by culturally autonomous regions, immigrant enclaves or neighborhoods and, finally, by discrete individuals. The intersection between these two dimensions minimally produces a 3 x 4 table such as that shown below:

10 Ethnolinguistic Democracy

Table. Interaction between Degree of Preferred Language Implementation and Scale of Political Power			
Preferred Language Implementation			
Scale	1. Full	2. Partial	3. Restricted
Between States	a1	a2	a3
Between States and Regions (Ss/Rs)	b1	b2	b3
Between Ss/Rs and Immigrant Neighborhoods	c1	c2	c3
Between Ss/Rs and "other ethnic" individuals	d1	d2	d3

Obviously, the above table can easily be extended by introducing refinements along both dimensions, but I propose to leave it as it now stands to facilitate a discussion of degrees and varieties of ethnolinguistic democracy and differing interpretations of a limit beyond which a certain advocated degree of ethnolinguistic democracy "can no longer be afforded."

Example 1. Complete Ethnolinguistic Democracy at the Interpolity Level (Cell a1)

As one might expect, the 12 members of the European (Economic) Community (hereafter EC) do not conduct themselves according to the usage of the "ethnic layer cake" empires of Eastern Antiquity. For the deliberations of the European Parliament in Strassburg, a parliament whose representatives are selected by means of formal elections conducted in each of the member countries, each of the nine state-building languages of the current twelve members are fully equal. Between pairs of these nine languages there are necessarily 72 directions of translation (9 x 8) because not only can all representatives address the Parliament in their own state language, but they can all hear the discussion in reply to any intervention in their own state language[2] as well. This arrangement guarantees that the representatives of the roughly two million Danish speakers do not need to be less secure nor be any more linguistically versatile than the representatives from England, France, or Germany. Granted that not every one of the above mentioned 72 directions of translation is equally common, and granted that in committee work or in documentary efforts (published or unpublished) a much smaller subset of languages is generally involved, the "principle of complete multilingualism" (this being the EC's designation of its own *organizational* operational pattern, rather than a characterization of the abilities of its *individual* delegates) remains dear to the heart of the initial 12 members of the EC, as we will see in connection with our discussion of cell b2, below.

Nevertheless, the future of the "principle of complete multilingualism" may well be a rather problematic one for the EC, even at the organizational level. With the Language Service already one of its largest budgetary items, how will the EC cope with the very probable expansion of its membership in the very near future? Sweden[3] is certainly assured of early membership, and Finland and Norway are almost in the same category. Membership for Hungary and Czechoslovakia (or separately for Bohemia-Moravia and Slovakia) is already under discussion. If the six state languages of these five (or six) additional prospective members are also to be treated as equal "in principle" with the current nine, that would result in 210 directions of translation between pairs of the 15 languages of 18 (or 19) members. If all the other pre-perestroika European states are ultimately admitted, i.e., even barring separate memberships for all of the recently independent subdivisions of the former Soviet and Yugoslav federations, the application of the principle of "complete multilingualism" would result in 420 directions of translation for official, parliamentary communication between 21 languages of 24 (or 25) members of a first approximation to an all-European EC.[4] If all the former Soviet and Yugoslav entities achieve separate membership, as now seems eminently possible within the next few years, that would result in 812 directions of translation between 29 languages of 33 (or 34) members![5] Clearly, sooner or later, some theory of limits must be invoked at the EC, but it is very difficult for sovereign states to agree to limit themselves, particularly when any such limitation not only contravenes a prior moral order but provides advantages to some members of the organization and denies them to others.[6]

Example 2. Partial Ethnolinguistic Democracy in Interactions between States and Regions (Cell b2)

The EC adopted its "principle of complete multilingualism" on December 11, 1990, i.e., relatively late in its own history and substantially later than the principle itself had begun to be implemented in its own operations (based as these operations were upon earlier, somewhat similar, principles and conventions). This principle was then newly defended and justified on the grounds that it was required in the light of "the respect which is owed the dignity of all languages which reflect and express the cultures of the different peoples who make up the European Community" (Argemi, 1991; Reding, 1990). However, some of "the different peoples who make up the European Community" are also and even more basically members of sub-state ethno-regional entities. These sub-state entities commonly have sub-state languages of their own. Do not these sub-state languages deserve some EC respect and recognition too? This very question was brought to a head by the newly autonomous Catalans in Spain, some six million strong, who brought a petition to the EC in 1987 signed by fully 100,000 individuals, requesting some sort of official standing in the EC for their language, a language of long-standing humanistic accomplishment and a language recognized as regionally co-official in Spain and spoken natively by more individuals than is the state language of Denmark. It was precisely the Catalan petition which finally moved the EC to proclaim that all European languages (by clear implication: even regional ones) deserved recognition so that "the people of Europe not come to regard European institutions as being out of touch with and foreign to them" but, rather, that they "look upon them as important elements playing a part in the daily lives of the citizens" (Argemi). In other words, the EC also implicitly applied its principle to the non-state-building peoples of the EC, rather than to the state-building peoples alone, precisely by reaffirming it in connection with the petition of a sub-state entity on behalf of its preferred language.

Nevertheless, it is noteworthy that even after the above truly sympathetic resolution, revealing as it does so much understanding of the ethnolinguistic sensitivities of regional language groups face to face with state languages in the New Europe, the EC still did not grant Catalan equal status within its parliamentary deliberations. In essence, in strictly operational organizational terms, the EC merely encouraged Catalan[7] to continue seeking some sort of other recognition, one that stops short of that now being implemented in connection with the nine current state-building languages. What might that "other recognition" amount to? It might very well be one which is reminiscent of a status that was operative in the ancient Empire of the Medes and the Persians, namely, the right to receive communications from the "center", or (as is more likely today) to send communications to the "center," in the language associated with regional identity and culture. The principle of ethnolinguistic democracy need not operate only and exclusively at the level of "complete multilingualism" via insisting that all languages be literally equally important and privileged for all functions. When the number of languages becomes *too great* (a judgmental, definitional matter indeed), some consideration of proportionality between languages may ultimately be appealed to and implemented. Some notion of limits must ultimately be appended to the notion of "complete (organizational) multilingualism," very much as notions of limits have existed in all theories of democracy and individual rights from the very earliest times (Fishman, in press). Cell b2 represents attempts to cope with this issue in a constructive way.

Just where and when the limits of democratic rights should be drawn, be they ethnolinguistic, econotechnical, or political, can well be viewed as a dilemma within the democratic ethos itself. Limits can obviously be set in self-serving ways and those who wield greater power are particularly likely to have a disproportionate say in the establishments of such limits for others. Establishments are more likely to limit others than to limit themselves. Establishments tend to appeal to or to implement any notion of limits primarily for the purpose of preserving and furthering their own power, rather than because some natural limit has truly been reached, on the one hand, or in order to engage in magnanimous power-sharing, on the other. Of course, the foregoing observations apply to *national* establishments at least as much as they apply to *international* establishments such as the EC.

Example 3. Restricted Ethnolinguistic Democracy:
A Problem of Immigrant Enclaves (Cell c3)

Living as we do in a period of American history when our central and local governmental authorities often communicate with (and even receive communications from) Hispanics, Amerindians, and various Asians in languages other than the main language of the state, we seldom pause to reflect how unusual such a convention is in historical and international perspective. Immigrant languages[8] are generally low on the totem-pole, and whatever recognition is given to them by the authorities is generally of a voluntary kind, i.e., not protected or required by law, and is therefore easily withdrawn or anulled at the whim of the authorities. It is not unusual throughout the world today to find that the most essential governmental services, such as police protection, fire protection, health care provision, legal proceedings in courts of law, elementary and secondary education (even if only for stipulated transitional periods), job training and retraining, and even citizenship training per se, are simply not available in other than the official, state-building languages. Although notable differences exist between them as to the extent of (and their statutory provisions for) ethnolinguistic democracy involving immigrant groups, Australia, the USA, and Western Europe are clearly unusual in this respect, even unusual in the perspective of the entire course of the history of those countries themselves. These countries (and a very few others elsewhere) constitute examples of the degree to which some notions of ethnolinguistic democracy have permeated Western standards of morality since the end of World War II, even if imperfectly so. The efforts of English Only/English Official protagonists in the USA (and of conservative groups, parties, and movements in Australia and Canada) may be viewed as seeking to return these few exceptional countries to their status quo ante, i.e., to move them from some point close to cell c2 ("partial ethnolinguistic democracy") to some point closer to c3 ("restricted ethnolinguistic democracy").

It should also be noted that immigrant groups are even more rarely assisted in any language-in-culture stabilization efforts that might tend to help them consolidate socioculturally over the long term. Such consolidation would, in essence, change immigrant groups from transient minorities (expected to transethnify and translinguify in the direction of the mainstream) into indigenized regional minorities such as the Tamils in Sri Lanka, the Jews in pre-World War II Eastern Europe and the Rusyns in Voyvodina. It is precisely the nativistic and ethnocentric fear of just such rare long-term developments that makes all but *restricted* ethnolinguistic democracy for immigrants the worldwide rule rather than the exception we have noted it to be in the few countries mentioned initially.

Example 4. Ethnolinguistic Rights for Individuals: The Territoriality and Personality Principles (Cells d1–d3)

The appeal to "reasonable limits" along the dimension of scale deals not only with the number of languages involved, as is the case with our EC examples, but also with the number of individuals involved. Often, even members of territorial (i.e., indigenous regional) minorities will be treated as foreign immigrants (or even worse) when encountered outside their legally defined regions. This is the case with francophones or italophones in German-speaking Switzerland, or of Walloons in the Flemish-speaking parts of Belgium. In both these instances, a rather pure and unadulterated territoriality principle is invoked and no ethnolinguistic democracy is accorded to such individuals outside their "proper" areas. Such neglect is essentially an example of cell d3 in operation. A more liberal policy has been encountered in India, where a "sufficient" number of speakers of "scheduled languages" can expect some governmental accommodation and consideration, even outside the linguistic states with which their languages are normally associated. USA Hispanics relocating in secondary settlement areas are also sometimes accommodated somewhat, merely because their more massive presence elsewhere within reach has resulted in Spanish-related personnel and materials being "tappable" in a pinch. A single Hispanic family in upper Maine may be in a much better situation than a single Hmong family in the identical location, but generally, what is involved when some such isolates are accommodated is the implementation of a much more restrictive arrangement which is much closer to cell d3 ("restricted ethnolinguistic democracy") than to cell d2 ("partial ethnolinguistic democracy").

Rare as examples of cell d2 are, examples of cell d1 are even rarer. It should come as no surprise that the co-occurence of full ethnolinguistic democracy and isolated individuals not speaking the dominant state-building language should be an obvious non-starter. The appearance of such individuals (particularly if they have no locally recognized territorial affiliations in an appropriate and nearby region) quickly galvanizes authorities to invoke a theory of limits and to provide, at best, only the most restricted type of emergency assistance. Furthermore, even such assistance as is provided tends to foster an image (with respect to those whose language is exceptionally recognized) of welfare recipients rather than that of co-equals and potential neighbors, friends, and co-citizens.

Parsimony and Ethnolinguistic Democracy

Ethnolinguistic democracy obviously involves a complex constellation of values which exact a price in time, effort, and resources. But there are no cost-free values. In terms of pure parsimony, it always appears to be easier, simpler, and cheaper to use just one or a very few major languages, regardless of individual or small-group ethnolinguistic sensitivities. The movements for one or another international auxiliary language are examples of the triumph of parsimony (or of a theory of limits) over the claims of ethnolinguistic democracy. Similarly, the operational policies of the United Nations or of the Council of Europe are also of this kind (both pertaining to cell a3), since they favor a very small sub-set of major, Western European languages—assumed to be "languages of wider communication" and, accordingly, presumably free of any "original sin," i.e., of "ethnic contamination." That such decontamination is purely perspectival and situational is obvious from the efforts by adherents of French, in particular, and of German, Italian, and Spanish to some extent as well, to keep English from being recognized as the *primus* (or *prima?*) *inter pares* that it has actually become in some EC operations. Thus parsimony of resources or the appeal to limits, as a tactic utilized in order to avoid the purportedly excessive costs engendered by *too many* small languages, this tactic itself runs into the counter-parsimony interests of those who are concerned with their own loss of status due to the selection of *too few* "super (i.e., super-power) languages." The latter counter-parsimony efforts are engaged in by polities that are ready, nay eager, to invoke the notion of limits against the sub-state languages in their own political orbit, while being extremely loathe to have the notion of limits applied above themselves, so to speak, at the level of supra-state organizations and activities. Although ethnolinguistic goals and claims are frequently and widely derided as self-seeking, it is often overlooked that the appeals to limits and to parsimony in linguistic affairs are similarly self-interest inspired and pack a considerably stronger wallop as well, being associated with the ethnolinguistic interests of the mightiest powers on the world arena. Because of their power, the linguistic Big Brothers deflect discussion of the costs to human creativity that would be occasioned by their restrictions of ethnolinguistic democracy under super-power tutelage. Seemingly, what is sauce for the goose is not sauce for the goslins in ethnolinguistic affairs.

Summary and Conclusions

I have tried to stress just a few major considerations throughout this presentation. Ethnolinguistic democracy is far from being an open-and-shut affair. There are different varieties, degrees, and even dimensions of ethnolinguistic democracy, and the entire notion is very perspectival in nature, even more so than most other value-laden societal phenomena, all of which tend to have a subjective component. Most states are prone to strive for more ethnolinguistic democracy at their own level, i.e., in inter-polity affairs, or at the level above their own, i.e., in supra-polity organizations. Conversely, they tend to be resistant to notions of ethnolinguistic democracy at the intra-state or sub-state level, due to their mistaken association of intra-polity linguistic heterogeneity with civil strife and with decreased per capita gross national product (Fishman, 1991). As a result of this mistaken association of intra-polity linguistic heterogeneity only with negative consequences, states (and their creations: interstate associations) are often, curiously enough, increasingly loathe to permit sub-state entities to enjoy full ethnolinguistic democracy, the further removed these entities are from already-recognized political and cultural self-regulation.

In an era in which intranational and international migrations are both at an all time high, sub-state ethnolinguistic democracy is therefore particularly in danger of being restricted. Similarly, as the Eastern European events of 1991 reveal, it also means that regions and groups striving toward the attainment of greater ethnolinguistic democracy may increasingly opt for regional autonomy and even political independence in order to attain ethnolinguistic security. However, if and when their independence is attained, the new polities that arise often tend to recapitulate the same types of negative ethnolinguistic approaches vis-à-vis their own minorities that were directed toward them, prior to their own attainment of self-regulation. All in all, *ethnolinguistic democracy tends to be pursued and advocated upward and denied and denigrated downward on the dimension of power and scale.*

In view of the foregoing circular developmental patterns, the reaffirmation of the "principle of complete multilingualism" by the European Community is particularly noteworthy, most particularly so as it pertains to and was brought about by a concern for sub-state languages. Although the European Community will necessarily need to move from "complete" toward "partial ethnolinguistic democracy," and to do so not only at the sub-state level but even at the interstate level (thereby tending to equalize the treatment that most state-building and all regional languages will receive in its operation), its legacy of championing the "dignity of all languages" and recognizing the need to make sure that people not come to regard the institutions that govern them "as being out of touch with and foreign to them," will remain noteworthy landmarks in supporting the strivings of little languages and peoples all over the world. If the European Community can hold the line for "moderate" or "partial" ethnolinguistic democracy, the benefits of that line will redound to the good of all of multicultural and multilingual humanity.

Western Europe was the original home from which political democracy, enlightenment rationalism, and ethnolinguistic romanticism (Fishman, 1972; Penrose and May, 1991) spread throughout the world. There is now reason to hope that the European Community's stance with respect to "complete ethnolinguistic democracy," and its predictable future stance on behalf of more moderate ethnolinguistic democracy, will enable this value cluster, too, to have more of a worldwide currency than it otherwise might. In a sense, a Western European debt may be being paid off in this connection. Europe (and Western Europe in particular) initially became more hostile to sub-state linguistic heterogeneity as its econotechnical and econopolitical development progressed. Perhaps its more recent *post*modern ability to compromise in this regard will be a harbinger of a greater willingness to do the same in Eastern Europe, in Africa, in Asia and, who knows, even in the Americas as well. *Ojala!* We must not let the recent multiplication of recognized state languages turn into a route for indigenous sub-state and foreign-derived immigrant tongues. The former does not have to be at the expense of the latter when partial ethnolinguistic democracy is seriously considered and honestly implemented.[9]

Notes

[1] Perhaps reference should be made here to "native" language or "mother tongue" because these expressions are so traditional and expected in connection with *ethno*linguistic concerns. More technically, however, the reference is often to the preferred language of ethnolinguistic identity and/or state functioning. The latter may not be the mother tongue at all for some segments of the population and at various stages of the total process of ethnolinguistic consciousness-raising, relinguification, and re-ethnification. In former publications I have used the expression "ethnic mother tongue" in this same extended sense, as distinguished from "actual mother tongue."

[2] Ireland has two official languages (Irish and English), but thus far, it has only asked that one of them (English) be recognized at the EC. Similarly, Luxembourg has requested no recognition for Letzeburgesch, implementing its EC membership entirely via French and German. Belgium's participation is effectuated via French and Netherlandish. The above three instances of states duplicating languages that would be represented at the EC even without the membership of these particular states, results in the above-mentioned totals of 12 member states but only 9 recognized languages in the EC as of April 1992.

[3] A Swedish linguist recently proposed that Sweden offer to forgo the use of Swedish at the EC, when its membership is approved, in order to lighten

the translation burdens of the organization and in view of the fact that its representatives will certainly all be fluent in either English, Danish, German or French (Suzanne Romaine, personal communication). This suggestion was met with an avalanche of rejection from a large and very vocal segment of Swedish society and it seems very unlikely that a newly admitted Sweden will now make any such unilateral self-denying gesture.

[4]The number 21 is arrived at by adding to the above 15 languages the following 6: Albanian, Bulgarian, Polish, Romanian, Russian, and Serbocroatian (considered as one language rather than as two).

[5]The number 29 is arrived at by adding to the above 21 the following 8 languages of 10 new member states: Croatian, Estonian, Latvian, Lithuanian, Macedonian, Moldavian, Slovenian, and Ukrainian. Serbia and Bosnia-Herzegovina are assumed to both opt for Serbian, while Croatian and Moldavian are considered to be different from Serbian and Romanian, respectively. Adding Armenian, Azerbaijani, and Georgian to the above list (assuming that their new polities seek a European rather than a trans-Caucasus affiliation) would bring the grand total to 32 languages and 992 (!) directions of translation between 36 (or 37) European states. Unmentioned, thus far, are Iceland (which would add yet another language) and Switzerland and Austria (which would not).

[6]Throughout this discussion I have ignored the problems of translation per se (e.g., costs, fidelity, translation-based miscommunication, etc.). The costs or "lost savings" attributable to ethnolinguistic democracy, as contrasted to the costs of (mis-)communicating via a shared second language such as Esperanto, have yet to be fully or accurately determined. Every human value, including ethnolinguistic democracy or parsimony, creates some problems as well as exacerbating and/or solving others.

[7]By implication, such other indigenous regional languages as Basque and Gallego in Spain, Alsatian, Breton, and Occitan in France, Frisian in the Netherlands, Sorbian in Germany, Friulian and Ladin in Italy, Romansch in Switzerland, Nynorsk and Sami in Norway, etc., might also consider themselves "encouraged" by the same resolution. These "Lesser Used Languages" are all within the purview of the EC's purely consultative "Bureau of Lesser Used Languages" (Jacoby, 1991 [?]).

[8]*Immigrant* languages are distinguished from *migrant* languages in the following remarks. Thus, neither English in Puerto Rico nor Russian in the Ukraine during the period of Soviet rule, are considered immigrant languages within the meaning of the term as used in this paper. Of course, a given language may switch in status from being immigrant to being an indigenous state or regional language after a judgmentally "sufficient" number of years has elapsed, viz. English in Ireland.

[9]Further evidence of the EC's continuing interest in regional and/or minority languages in Europe, with the goal of preparing and adopting a

"European Charter for Regional or Minority Languages," is available in the reports of March 26 [CAHLR (92) 5] and April 1 [CAHLR (92) 6], 1992, of its Ad Hoc Committee of Experts on Regional or Minority Languages in Europe. I am indebted to Dr. Donall O Riagain, secretary general of the EC-affiliated European Bureau for Lesser Used Languages, for providing me with copies of all the above.

References

Argemi, Aureli. "European Recognition for Catalan," *Contact: Bulletin of the European Bureau for Lesser Used Languages* 8.1 (1991): 6.
Coulmas, Florian, ed. *A Language Policy for the European Community: Prospects and Quandaries*. Berlin: Mouton de Gruyter, 1991.
Fishman, Joshua A. "An Inter-Polity Perspective on the Relationship between Linguistic Heterogeneity, Civil Strife and Per Capita Gross National Product." *International Journal of Applied Linguistics* 1 (1991): 5-18.
———. *Language and Nationalism*. Rowley, MA: Newbury, 1972. Also reprinted in Fishman, *Language and Ethnicity in Minority Ethnolinguistic Perspective*. Clevedon: Multilingual Matters, 1989. 105-75 and 269-367.
———. "On the Limits of Ethnolinguistic Democracy." In *Linguistic Human Rights* Ed. T. Skutnabb-Kangas and Robert Phillips. (In press).
Haarmann, Harald. "Monolingualism vs. Selective Multilingualism: On the Future Alternatives for Europe as It Integrates in the 1990s." *Sociolinguistica* 5 (1991): 7-23.
Haselhuber, Jakob. "Erste Ergebnisse einer empirischen Untersuchung zur Sprachsituation in der EG-Komission (February 1960)." *Sociolinguistica* 5 (1991): 37-50.
Jacoby, Lucien. *European Community Activity in Favor of Lesser Used Languages and Cultures, 1983-1989*. Baile Atha Cliath/Wilwerwitz, European Bureau for Lesser Used Languages, 1991(?).
Leitner, Gerhard. "Europe 1992: A Language Perspective." *Language Problems and Language Planning* 15 (1991): 282-96.
Penrose, Jan, and Joe May. "Herder's Concept of Nation and its Relevance to Contemporary Ethnic Nationalism." *Canadian Review of Studies in Nationalism* 18 (1991): 179-86.
Reding, V. Report drawn up on behalf of the Committee on Petitions. Strasbourg, European Parliament.; Session Documents: DOC EN/RR/ 87761. 1990.
Turi, G. "The Right to Language; The Value of Esperanto." *The New Party* 26.7 (1992): 11.

Is Linguistic Evolution in the United Nations a Consequence of Recent Political Evolution?

Jean Gazarian

Pour pouvoir communiquer notre pensée par l'intermédiaire d'une langue, il faut comme condition préalable que nos interlocuteurs aient une connaissance suffisante de cette langue. C'est pourquoi, à mon grand regret, je vais devoir abandonner provisoirement la langue de Molière, car je crois comprendre que certains de nos lecteurs ne la maîtrisent pas encore.

Following the example of the Canadian diplomats, whose speeches are delivered partly in English and partly in French, the two official languages of their country, I shall switch from my native language to the other working language of the United Nations Secretariat out of consideration for those whose French is still a bit deficient.

It is well known that over the centuries, in trying to assert their authority over their own subjects or the inhabitants of the lands they had conquered, the leaders of the most powerful countries tended to impose their own rule. In doing so, they would invariably promote and often impose the use of their national language. Hence the preponderance of Greek in ancient times, followed by the extensive use of Latin in the vast Roman empire. For many centuries, Latin remained the language of scholars and, until recently, the universal language of the Roman Catholic Church.

In more recent times, several European countries (Belgium, Denmark, England, France, Germany, Holland, Italy, Portugal, and Spain), to which one should add Japan, the Ottoman Empire, and Russia, conquered vast territories either near their borders or in remote parts of the world. In the name of civilization or, more exactly, for the sake of uniformity, the rulers of those countries often tried to impose their own language as the official language of the conquered lands. That decision was often dictated by the absence of a single language that could be used in the colonized territories as a common means of communication.

When the League of Nations was established after the First World War, English and French were recognized as its two official languages. At the time, French enjoyed a predominant role as the traditional language of diplomacy, and the new organization was situated in a French-speaking environment.

When the representatives of 51 states signed the Charter of the United Nations at San Francisco in June, 1945, they were approving a binding instrument, most of which had been drafted before the end of the Second World War. It is therefore not surprising that in the Charter special consideration was given to the Allied Powers. Thus, four of the official languages in which the Charter was adopted and signed (Chinese, English, French, and Russian) were the national languages of the permanent members of the Security Council, which had been given primary responsibility for the maintenance of international peace and security. The fifth language (Spanish) was obviously included because of the large number of Spanish-speaking Latin American republics, which at the time represented more than one third the total membership of the United Nations.

By a resolution adopted in February 1946, the General Assembly decided that the five languages of the Charter would become the official languages of all the principal organs of the United Nations.[1] The Assembly also decided that English and French would be the working languages of all the principal organs, which required all texts to be published in those two languages. Not a language of the Charter, Arabic was added as an official language of the United Nations in 1980.[2] Although not adopted as an official language, German is a language of publication for some important documents, such as resolutions of the General Assembly and the annual report of the Secretary General.

At present Arabic, Chinese, English, French, Russian, and Spanish are the working languages of the General Assembly and the Security Council. English, French, and Spanish are the working languages of the Economic and Social Council. English and French are the working languages of the Trusteeship Council, the International Court of Justice, and the Secretariat.

The equality of the two working languages of the Secretariat has often been emphasized by the Secretaries General. In a recent communication to the permanent missions of all member and observer states, the Secretary General drew their attention to the importance of languages as a means of communication:

> The working languages of United Nations peace-keeping operations are English and French, plus, in some cases, another of the Organization's official languages.... Inability to communicate in one of the Mission's working languages, to understand instructions, whether written or oral, and to gather and exchange information in that language is particularly damaging to the ability of police personnel to carry out their functions, which almost always require rapid and accurate oral communication.

Delegates to the General Assembly may use any of the six working languages. During the general debate of the Assembly's 1992 session, which included 167 speeches by heads of state, heads of government, ministers for foreign affairs, and other dignitaries, the allocation of official languages was as follows:

Use of Official Languages by the UN General Assembly, 1992		
Language	No. of Delegations	Percentage of Delegations
English	68	41%
French	31	19%
Spanish	20	12%
Arabic	18	10.5%
Russian	7	4%
Chinese	1	0.5%
English and French	1	0.5%

The percentage figures clearly demonstrate that this allocation accounts for just over 87% of these speeches (146 of 167). Under the rules of procedure, delegates have the option to use a language other than an official language if they provide interpretation into one of the official languages. During the general debate, 21 speakers (12.5%) availed themselves of this option, the highest percentage ever to do so. They represented the following countries:

Angola	Latvia
Brazil	Lithuania
Cape Verde	Mongolia
Croatia	Portugal
Democratic People's Republic of Korea	Republic of Korea
	San Marino
Germany	São Tome and Principe
Indonesia	
Iran	Slovenia
Italy	Tajikistan
Japan	Ukraine
Lao People's Democratic Republic	

This trend is definitely new and significant. For lack of fluency in any of the United Nations official languages or, more likely, for reasons of prestige or internal consumption, an increasing number of delegates have decided to use their national language.

This list leads us directly to another observation concerning the former Soviet Union. As may be expected, the representatives of most of the republics of the former USSR that participated in the general debate expressed themselves in Russian (Azerbaijan, Belarus, Georgia, Kazakhstan, Kyrgyzstan, the Russian Federation, and Uzbekistan), but seven of them decided to use another language: some chose French (Armenia and Moldova), English (Estonia), or their national language (Latvia, Lithuania, Tajikistan, and Ukraine). By not using Russian, in which they were undoubtedly most fluent, the representatives of these seven republics wanted to assert their newly acquired independence.

I have endeavored to present some arguments to support the thesis that a linguistic evolution in the United Nations is a consequence of international political evolution. To a great extent, this theme is justified. Over the centuries, major rulers in the world have used their vantage point to force the inhabitants of the lands they conquered to use the language of the occupying power. But they were not always successful. In spite of its centralized authority and obvious determination to promote the use of Russian, the Soviet Union understood the need to grant linguistic concessions to the various components of the Union. Thus, the constitutions of the Soviet republics usually provided for the coexistence of two languages: Russian and the national language of the republic.

One of the purposes of the United Nations, as enshrined in its Charter, is to

> achieve international cooperation in solving international problems of an economic, social, cultural or humanitarian character, and in promoting and encouraging respect for human rights and for fundamental freedoms for all without distinction as to race, sex, language or religion.[3]

As our forefathers proclaimed it almost half a century ago, let us hope that freedom of expression will prevail, that no multilingual nation or organization will ever be forced, for political or other reasons, to use only one language.

For centuries, French was the diplomatic language *par excellence*. The addition of English as an official language of the League of Nations did not impoverish the League; far from it. Similarly, the six working languages of the General Assembly and the Security Council contribute significantly, in their respective ways, to the wealth of our unique World Organization.

As a citizen of France, I now have a passport that reads "Communauté européenne—République Française" with inscriptions in ten languages. I fully realize that the proliferation of languages in a society can be costly and cumbersome, but I am convinced that the forced suppression of languages would engender intellectual poverty.

Diversity should not be eliminated. There can be no floral arrangement without a variety of flowers, no crown without an assortment of jewels, and no mosaic without a multitude of stones. There should be a linguistic evolution at the national and international levels, but it should result from free choice and never be dictated by authoritarian rule. Peruvians have chosen Spanish as their national language, Brazilians Portuguese, Senegalese French, and Americans English. They have enriched those languages with many local expressions. Yet, they could have followed a different course. In several independent countries, the language of the former rulers has almost entirely disappeared. This is the way it should be: freedom of choice, free linguistic evolution irrespective of political evolution. In every case, *vox populi* ought to prevail.

Notes

[1] Resolution 2(I) of 1 February 1946.
[2] Resolutions 35/219A and B of 17 December 1980.
[3] Charter of the United Nations, Chapter I, Purposes and Principles, Article 1, paragraph 3.

Changes in the Pattern of Language Use in the United Nations

Stephen B. Pearl

It is acknowledged on all hands that there is a New World Political Order, and new orders are very much the order of the day, generated and nurtured as they are by a largely third-world sense of grievance against the old orders imposed by the world's richer, more powerful, and predominantly European nations. By contrast, the linguistic order inherited by the United Nations from its rich, powerful, industrialised, and predominantly European founders has been accepted with astonishingly little dissent by that very third-world majority which labours under its disadvantages. From the same folks who brought us the New World Economic Order and the New World Information Order we hear little or nothing about the need for a New World Linguistic Order.

Why is it assumed that a multinational organisation must be multilingual? Firstly, because not everyone speaks the same language and secondly, even if they could all be persuaded to speak the same language, the choice of that language would be invidious and unfair to the speakers of other languages. While both of these propositions are true, it is equally true that not everyone thinks of the same 5 or 6, or even 7, 8, or 9 languages and that even if everyone could be persuaded to speak one of those 5 to 9 languages, the choice of those languages would be equally invidious, and it would still not be fair to speakers of other languages.[1]

Having raised these larger questions, including that of whether making everyone speak the same one language is more or less fair to more or fewer people or countries than making everyone speak one of a limited number of languages as well as the question of whether the existing dispensation is the most rational, efficient, and economically possible and whether these considerations are rightly subordinated to respect for political and national sensibilities, I shall tiptoe around the polemical minefield of an attempt to answer them.

Unlegislated and spontaneous changes in the patterns of language use within the world organisation have certainly been taking place, and it may be that they can perfectly well be contained and accommodated within the existing language dispensation without bursting the envelope—perhaps another historical example of room for evolution preempting revolution—and I shall attempt to account for some of these changes.

Translation and interpretation are established facts of life at the UN and other international organisations, and if anyone were to ask why, the reply would no doubt be "so that speakers and writers of different languages can understand each other." The respondent would no doubt be wondering privately how anyone could even ask such a dumb question. Individuals and institutions, especially, have a tendency to deduce what ought to be from what is, and it is axiomatic that in an organisation in which representatives of different nations speak mutually unintelligible languages and need to understand and be understood by each other, some means will be required to satisfy that need. The truth is that in the UN and other international organisations, there has been a reversal of cause and effect and that instead of translation and interpretation satisfying an existing need, it is the need itself which is created by the existence of the means to satisfy it—a perversity not unknown in the production and consumption of consumer goods. This truth is obscured partly by the human and institutional tendency I have mentioned and partly by a failure to distinguish clearly between *nations* where certain languages are spoken and the *individuals* representing those nations who actually speak (and listen) in the UN. So while it is true that Albanian is the language spoken in Albania and that this fact creates a linguistic need to be met by facilities for translation and interpretation from and into Albanian, this need is no more or less compelling than that created by the fact that Russian is the language spoken in Russia. However, whether or not translation and interpretation to and from Albanian is provided at the UN is not dictated by the need for it; rather, the fact that Albanian is *not* spoken at the UN is the *effect* of the fact that the facilities for it are *not* provided. Similarly, the fact that Russian *is* spoken at the UN is the *effect* of providing the necessary facilities, not the cause of providing them.

In other words, the Albanian foreign ministry simply sends representatives to the UN who can speak and understand one of the official languages because no facilities exist for the translation and interpretation of Albanian. The Russian foreign ministry sends representatives who may need translation and interpretation to and from that language because the facilities exist. I say "may need" because it has become less and less likely over the years that Russia or indeed any of the countries who enjoy the privilege of being able to use their own languages at the UN will send individuals here to represent them who actually need to use their own language any more than the representatives of Myanmar or Poland need to use theirs.

I have used "less and less likely" to mark a distinct evolution in language use at the UN. What may have started life as a need—in the highly relative sense I have explained, a need which disappears if the means to satisfy it are lacking and vice versa—is now evolving into an option or a privilege to be exercised as representatives choose, whether as speakers or listeners. This evolution needs to be discussed within the whole framework of the changing pattern of language use in the UN.

I should qualify this evolution by drawing a distinction between the more visible political and diplomatic discussion and debate that goes on in the UN and its less accessible and submerged underside. This qualification applies particularly to the New York-based activities. The political hub of the organisation, New York gets the lion's share of media coverage, partly because it is in the USA. It is unlikely that you will ever see outside the meeting room in the Palais des Nations in Geneva where they are discussing the standardization of perishable foodstuffs or deep-mined coal anything approaching the piranha-like feeding frenzy which grips the media representatives milling hungrily outside the Security Council consultation room in New York when the doors open and yet another hapless ambassador is tossed out into their midst.

The regularly accredited career diplomats at the UN are less and less likely to need translation and interpretation facilities for their own languages, if they exist. But such multilingualism is less likely to be found among experts in various fields who are sent to meetings on technical and semi-technical subjects, and it is here that the linguistic privileges enjoyed by some countries are perhaps most valuable and, if you like, most unfair. Denied by definition to a majority of member states, this privilege compounds the constraint of subject-matter expertise: in the main, precisely the bigger countries, whose languages are spoken at the UN, are those likely to have a larger choice of experts at their bidding and are not limited in their choice of expert by his or her proficiency in foreign languages. The smaller and poorer countries, whose choice is already limited to the very few experts they may have in, say, the desalination of sea water or the effects of atomic radiation, find their choice further limited to a representative who can or claims to be able to express himself in one of the official UN languages. In the case of representatives of smaller, especially third world, countries attending meetings of expert and technical bodies, it may well be even more important for their representatives to be able to understand an official language than to express themselves in it. The role and purpose of technical or expert bodies varies acording to the subject and mandate, but by and large, the airing and sharing of state-of-the-art knowledge and information is key. Usually the representatives of the smaller and poorer countries are at the receiving end of this exchange. Only if the listener can follow and understand the speaker in the language spoken or in one of the languages into which it is interpreted, will he benefit from it. Simultaneous interpretation, however, is by no means the medium of choice for conveying technical information and exchanges between experts, for all that it may be blithely and unquestioningly assumed to be.

My assertion that over the years, representatives at the UN from the linguistically privileged countries have become less and less likely to need, and hence to use, the translation and interpretation facilities provided for their languages deserves some explanation. Delegations have become increasingly aware that it may be a mixed blessing to speak one's own language or to listen to interpretation into it. The present permanent representative of Hungary is a man of remarkable linguistic accomplishments. When I first met him, he was speaking Russian, and I would not have taken him for anything but a native speaker of that language. When I remarked that I had never heard him speak Russian at the UN, he replied that he preferred to speak French because he felt that it gave him direct access to a wider audience. Knowing that he also speaks English, I asked him why he did not take the next logical step and speak English, thus gaining direct access to by far the largest audience. He replied that he felt more at home in French than in English. Not every delegate is as sensitive to this factor of direct access to his listeners, but then not every delegate is fortunate or accomplished enough to be able to do something about it even when using his own language. Hungarian, in this instance, is not an available option. However, an increasing number of delegates who have the privilege of speaking and listening to their own language are not exercising this option, particularly in less formal and ceremonial meetings. The increasing willingness and ability of such delegates to speak and listen to an official UN language other than their own—in nine cases out of ten, delegates from Arabic-, Chinese-, Russian-, Spanish-, and even French-speaking countries speaking and listening to English—has been accompanied by another evolution, namely the rise in the practice of informal consultations.

These two interactive factors have themselves markedly affected the overall pattern of language use in UN meetings in favour of English and away from the other official languages. This change would not be apparent to visitors to the UN or to the public at large whose access is restricted to the visible tip of the iceberg of UN meeting activity—a tip whose size has remained relatively constant while the whole mass of the iceberg has swollen considerably. The consequent redistribution of language use has had a much greater impact on interpretation than on translation. In the less formal meetings, now much more numerous, apart from the willingness and ability of delegates to speak English in preference to their own official language, another factor reinforces this trend and has to do with group dynamics. As meetings get under way, delegates who may have started out speaking Arabic, Chinese, Russian, Spanish, or even French become influenced, encouraged, or even challenged by the example of others switching from their own languages to English and begin to follow suit. This trend was set much earlier and has been followed even more consistently by secretariat officials themselves who have occasion to address intergovernmental bodies. What may have started out as individual preferences on the part of secretariat officials now seems to have hardened into something like policy, and only rarely do such officials prefer their own—when they happen to be UN—languages to English. This practice has no doubt made its own contribution to creating a general climate of anglo-saxophony.

In any case, because of the informality and size of the meeting (the smaller the numbers, the stronger the tendency), there is the same trend towards a single lingua franca that occurs in private gatherings of individuals of different language backgrounds. The Security Council itself is a paradigm and has been the trend setter in this development.

Twenty-five to thirty years ago practically all its work was conducted in public. The proceedings were contentious, confrontational, and protracted; tirades and harangues sparked angry rights of reply. Indignation, outrage, and denunciation, expressed exclusively in the speaker's own working language, were the order of the day. Every issue was refracted through the prism of the Cold War. Although there had always been some meetings behind closed doors between some members of the Council, it was only when Arthur Goldberg came to the UN as US ambassador, bringing with him a reputation as an effective and successful labour-management arbitrator, that the practice was begun of trying to hammer out compromise among Security Council members behind closed doors, away from the heat and glare of the public arena. Later, a fully equipped consultation room was built, thus consecrating and institutionalising the practice of informal consultations of the whole membership.

With the end of colonialism, the winding down of the Cold War under Gorbachev, and finally the demise of the Soviet Union and with it the end of East-West confrontation, the work of the Council has taken on a completely different complexion and is conducted largely out of public sight and earshot. Public meetings of the Council now serve almost exclusively to formalize the consensus or compromise that has been worked out in private. Inside the consultation room where there is no public opinion to influence, inflame, or play to, argument has replaced rhetoric, and even at formal meetings, it is rare to hear anything more turbulent than straightforward statements of position or explanations of vote, if only because by this stage the issue has almost always been resolved and no delegation's vote is any longer "up for grabs."

This practice of the Security Council has now spread to practically every other body in the UN, and there are now creatures known as "informal informals" that can subsist on a diet of "non-papers" without a USDA-prescribed minimum daily allowance of simultaneous interpretation.

In discussing the evolution—practically a revolution—in the proceedings of the Security Council, I have grazed the question of "influencing votes." Each member state defends and promotes its national interests through its votes on the various resolutions and its attempts to influence the votes of others. The heads of delegations to the UN are known as permanent representatives, and members of delegations are often thought of and described as representatives of their countries, but their role and function should not be confused with that of "representatives" in the US Congress or deputies or members of parliament of national legislatures. Unlike members of these bodies who, for good or ill, have achieved varying degrees of independence from both their constituents and their parties and still less like members of a jury, answerable to nobody but themselves for the way they vote, delegates are not sent to the UN to decide how to vote but to *cast* the vote of their government, undoubtedly a step up from a somewhat older definition of a diplomat's function: "an honest man sent abroad to lie for the good of his country." No matter how spellbinding the rhetoric or how compelling the case, those who make policy back in their capitals are simply not present to be swayed by oratory, while the representatives who are present and might be influenced are bound by instructions from their governments. Abba Eban who at one time represented Israel at the UN was widely acknowledged even by his country's adversaries as a Demosthenes, but the only harvest ever reaped by even his highest flights of eloquence were overwhelming majorities against his country.Ultimately it is perhaps by this criterion or "bottom line" that the "fairness" of the UN language dispensation should be measured.

Certainly, at one level, a minority of delegates, the linguistic "haves," do enjoy the privilege of arguing their cause in their own languages and delegates who do not share this privilege, the "have nots," do labour under a sometimes severe, subjective disadvantage in presenting their cases and rebutting those of others; they may very well end up presenting them badly and at times well nigh incomprehensibly. Objectively, at the level of the "bottom line," it does not matter because the actual voting on the isssue will be dictated by instructions from capitals and not by the extent to which delegates may have been impressed or convinced by each other's advocacy.

To the extent that delegates have career interests which can be advanced by their performance at the UN, command of language and powers of expression can certainly help commend them to fellow delegates. Along with other factors, such as the political acceptability of the countries they represent, this qualification can play a role in their election to honorific positions such as chairmanships of various UN bodies. In turn, such chairmanships give delegates an opportunity to display further potentially career-enhancing qualities and "make a name for themselves." It would take a much more detailed analysis to determine whether in fact the linguistic playing field is really level for all delegates in this regard.

I have mentioned a growing willingness and ability on the part of delegates to speak English in the UN in preference to their own official languages, thus placing themselves on the same de facto footing as many of their colleagues whose first language is not one of the official languages. I say "to speak English" because the traffic is almost exclusively one way. It is the rarest of exceptions for a representative of a country whose official language is English to venture a comment in Arabic, Chinese, French, Russian, or Spanish, and it is not without significance that these rare forays tend to be undertaken in a spirit of "cuteness" and greeted with a ripple of merriment. Freud is not alone among theorists of laughter in associating it with the "untoward."

One potent factor in this evolution has to do with a change in the perception on the part of governments of the role and function of the UN as a meeting place. It seemed that in the early days, governments tended to take the UN at face value as a multilateral, multilingual forum whose primary function was debate and to which, all other things being equal, you would want to send your best debaters. It is no coincidence that the first two decades of the UN yielded a score or more of men who were and thought of themselves as orators. Names such as Krishna Menon, Andrei Vyshinsky, Paul Henri Spaak, Adlai Stevenson, and Abba Eban leap to mind, and it is worth noting that all of these shared the privilege of being able to express themselves in their first language—not always the official language of the country they represented! The last two decades have seen their share of effective and lucid speakers, but none who could even take the field against the giants of yore.

Over the years, governments have increasingly come to realise that votes are not so much influenced by oratory in public debate but rather garnered by bilateral or, for want of a better word, "paucilateral" dealings behind the scenes. In this environment, like some hypertrophied dinosaur, the orator has outlived his usefulness, and if, as tended to be the case, he was an actual or virtual monoglot in a language other than English or, to a certain extent, French, his usefulness as a one-on-one negotiator was severely limited. As their practice has shown, more and more countries—both the linguistic "haves" and "have nots"—are sending to the UN representatives who can operate in English and the momentum gathered by this trend has become almost irresistible. As more and more delegates transact their business in English, it becomes ever more essential for countries to send delegates linguistically equipped to do business with their colleagues.

This change in perception and its effect on language use in the UN has been reinforced by a series of generational, social, and political factors. In the early sixties, there were considerably more delegates who could safely be relied upon to speak French and, paradoxical as it might seem now that the former Russian-speaking USSR has broken up into 15 new sovereign states most of whom are represented in the UN, quite a few more who could be expected to speak Russian.

For some 25 years, representatives of Arabic-speaking countries spoke either French or English, depending on the cultural influence bequeathed to their countries by the former colonial or quasi-colonial powers. Although Arabic has now become an official language, it is the only one to have been grafted onto a strong pre-existing pattern of language use, whereby generations of delegates from Arabic-speaking countries had come to feel thoroughly at home using French or English. Consequently, among these delegations there is an even more pronounced tendency to reserve the use of Arabic for the more formal and ceremonial occasions. For example, the Egyptian ambassador, who presides very comfortably and ably in English over the committee discussing the secretary general's Agenda for Peace, even responding in English when addressed in Arabic, in December 1992 spoke Arabic in the formal debate in the Plenary of the General Assembly on Bosnia and Herzegovina. How conscious he may have been of not having direct access to the widest audience I do not know, but the anglophone audience was hearing him at two removes, via interpretation from Arabic into French and via "relay" from French into English.[2]

Among those representatives who could be expected to speak French were fellow French speakers from Belgium, fellow Romance speakers from Italy and Romania, Balkan and Middle European carriers of an older European cosmopolitan culture from such countries as Albania, Greece, Turkey, and even Finland, the sole Western Hemisphere francophone,[3] Haïti, and those from the former French colonial territories in sub-Saharan Africa, North Africa, the Levant, and South East Asia, as and when they began to join the UN. Since the total membership was much smaller in those days and the absolute number of French speakers was higher, the proportion of French spoken was that much greater.

As for Russian, apart from Byelorussia, Ukraine, and the USSR, Mongolia and Albania, until its falling out with the USSR, when it switched abruptly to French, were also virtually Russian-speaking delegations.

Other Slavic-speaking delegates, particularly the Bulgarian, were as likely as not to speak Russian in addition to other non-Slavic members of the Eastern European bloc such as the GDR, Hungary, and Romania. Indeed, one of the last representatives of the GDR, Ambassador Florin, spoke Russian much more consistently throughout his tenure than did a number of his Soviet colleagues, and it was by no means unknown for an exchange to be conducted in, for example, the informal consultations of the Security Council by him in Russian and by his Soviet colleague in English.

Although the group of actual and potential Russian-speaking delegations was never numerically large, the amount of Russian spoken during the Cold-War period was out of all proportion to these numbers and was dictated by the dynamics of confrontation. It would only be a slight exaggeration to say that practically any position taken in any forum on any issue with even remotely political implications by US or Western delegations was strenuously and vociferously opposed by the Eastern side, predominantly in Russian. The converse was also true, especially when the USSR came up with its numerous initiatives in the field of international peace and security and disarmament. For years, a forum like the Trusteeship Council was the arena for endless recriminatory cut and thrust with the Soviet delegation doing most of the cutting and thrusting and the Western colonial powers in the dock.

Although there has been no major political shift in the role and position of the Spanish-speaking delegations, there has been a shrinkage in the proportion of Spanish-speaking delegations to the whole membership. The accretion to the ranks of English- and French-speaking delegations generated by the end of colonialism has been matched by the lone addition of Equatorial Guinea to the Spanish-speaking ranks. The number of these delegations which originally accounted for some 20 out of a total membership of 50+, has increased by one, while the total membership has climbed to some 180. However, a mixture of generational, social, and geographical factors, some of which have also affected the users of the other official UN languages to varying degrees, have had a notable impact on the language use of Latin American delegations.

Because of the proximity of their hemispheric, super-power neighbour and its economic and cultural drawing power, and because Latin American diplomatic services tend to draw their recruits from a social elite (a practice not restricted to Latin America), one rarely finds a member of the new generation of Latin American diplomats at the UN who has not received at least part of his or her higher education, and indeed secondary education, at an English-speaking institution. Consequently in the less formal meetings, more and more Latin American delegates are speaking English, and, of perhaps more significance for language services, are listening to that language more frequently. Not only is English being used increasingly by the linguistic "haves" as well as the "have nots," but it is becoming an even more widely "listened to" language. One of the reasons derives from the same linguistic bandwagon effect I have mentioned. As English becomes more of a de facto lingua franca, more and more delegates who do not and may never actually use it at meetings, listen to it in meetings in order to improve their knowledge and understanding of it and also because, just as Ambassador Erdös of Hungary felt more comfortable using French because it gives him direct access to a wider audience, so do many delegates feel more comfortable and more "in touch" if they can listen directly to the speaker.

40 Changes in the Pattern of Language Use

Another evolution within the UN affecting the absolute volume and the proportion of French and Spanish spoken at meetings has been the marked falling off of caucus meetings, an evolution itself reflecting geopolitical shifts and realignments. When the non-aligned movement was in its heyday, meetings of the non-aligned group at the UN were far more frequent, lengthy, and boisterous, as were meetings of the African group, the Afro-Asian group, the Asian group, and the Latin American group (now the group of Latin American and Caribbean states). The proportion of French spoken in the African group, Spanish in the Latin American group, and French and Spanish in the non-aligned group, from which the major European powers and the US were excluded, was naturally greater than in meetings of the whole membership. As the Romans used to say, or as at least one Roman, who obviously did not have verbatim records in mind at the time, once wrote: "Verba volant, scripta manent," and this very real but evanescent fact of linguistic life at the UN is one more factor unlikely to be reflected in any records or to have left any trace in the work of translation.

Along with this evolution, there has been a marked reduction in the number of countries whose representatives can be expected to speak French. While the former French sub-Saharan colonies have remained within the francophone fold, the former Southeast Asian colonies—Laos, Cambodia, and Vietnam—have largely strayed from it and now, partly, no doubt, for generational reasons, have embraced English. The former Maghreb colonies—Morocco, Tunisia, and even Algeria—are now as likely to speak English as French, while Syria and Lebanon, when not speaking Arabic, are even more likely to use English, especially in less formal contexts.

Even before the demise of the USSR, the detente ushered in by glasnost and perestroika had brought with it a marked decline in confrontational rhetoric and hence in the volume of Russian heard at the UN. The break-up of the Soviet Union into 15 new sovereign states has not, as some might have expected, brought 14 new Russian-speaking delegations to the UN, thus leading to a net increase in the volume of Russian. In actual fact, the shrinkage has been remarkable. The post-confrontational factor plays its part, of course, but the principal factor is the overwhelming priority of agonising domestic problems which has driven international and UN-related issues way down to the bottom of the agenda. This low profile would undoubtedly be reflected in a comparison between the number of people who remember the name Shevardnadze and the number who could tell you the name of the current Foreign Minister of the Russian Federation. As for the other former republics, few of their delegations are fully manned or exerienced and some, such as Ukraine and the Baltic States, for their own reasons, have so far shown a notable lack of enthusiasm for using Russian. At a recent meeting of a working group of the Fifth Committee of the General Assembly on the scale of assessments, the various linguistic and extra-linguistic factors at work produced a scenario in which the representative of the Russian Federation spoke English in spite of being far from at home in the language. English was also spoken by the representatives of the Baltic States, while Belarus and Kazakhstan spoke Russian. At present it seems that of the former Soviet republics, it is Kazakhstan which is the most immune to the the various Russo-fugal and Anglo-petal forces at work.

Suppose that all the rooms in the UN Building in New York had, for whatever reason, been fitted with doorways only 5 feet, 6 inches in height, it would have become "necessary" for member states to send only short diplomats to represent them at the UN. The longer the "doorway dispensation" was accepted as a fact of UN life and complied with by member states, the more "normal" and "natural" and unquestioned it would have become, until the day that an authoritative voice pointed out that it was only really "necessary" for delegates to be short because no one had questioned the "necessity" for the low doorways. Of course, countries where the average height was greater would have been penalised by this limitation especially in the technical and semi-technical meetings where their best experts were six-footers, but then again it would have created more openings in international diplomacy for retired jockeys.

Whatever arguments there may be for or against keeping the UN multilingual, going megalingual like the European Community, or paring it down to the linguistic bone, there is a powerful public relations aspect which should not be overlooked, an aspect, moreover, with financial implications. I do not know how much income is generated by the visitors' service, but like a panda in a zoo which always attracts many more visitors than would otherwise be interested in a zoo per se, the fact that many languages are spoken (and above all simultaneously interpreted) invests the UN as an institution with an intrigue and glamour that makes it interesting to a great many even quite sophisticated people, as well as lending an edge to the drawing power of some of its high-profile debates as media events.

Notes

[1] Of all the world's thousands of languages only six are official languages of the United Nations: Arabic, Chinese, English, French, Russian, and Spanish.

[2] Interpretation is not always accomplished directly from one language into another. Since the number of possible combinations of source and target languages can only be fully accommodated by hiring interpreters for each possible combination, less-frequent combinations are subject to interpretation into one of the most frequently used languages, which other staff then use as the source language for interpretation into another target language. Cf. Fishman in this volume.

[3] During the period under discussion, Canadian representatives rarely used French.

The Role of Russian in the Post-Cold-War Era

Alexandre K. Titov

The rumors about the untimely demise of Russian as one of the official and working languages at the United Nations —so irresponsibly spread by some newspapers and unwisely fanned by some officials—are, to paraphrase the well-known words of Mark Twain, highly exaggerated.

Welcome to the 21st century. It seems to have arrived sooner than anyone expected. Everything happens fast. We seem to live in an age of change, in which virtually everything is changing, including the nature of change itself. The Cold War has ended, just like that. It did not happen in the classic 20th-century fashion, with planes dropping loads of bombs that killed thousands of people. Instead, civilians went out and knocked down the Berlin Wall.

The unparalleled dramatic changes in the world were caused by profound transformations, initiated in the former Soviet Union under the slogan of "perestroika." In the United Nations, from the rostrum of the General Assembly, the then-Secretary General of the then-Communist Party of the then-Soviet Union, Mr. Gorbachev, delivered, in Russian, his famous speech of December 1988 that marked the beginning of a new era.

The 20th century has been the age of Orwellian institutions—states, corporations, bureaucracies—that control information. The individual has had increasingly narrow access to unbiased and unmotivated information. And this is one of the crucial points in the approach to the role of the Russian language. Cultural revolution, literacy for millions of people, free access to education at all levels, national universities for people who didn't have their alphabet or written history of cultural experience just several decades before, emergence and growth of national cultural awareness and identity—all these were elements of an undeniable success of new Soviet power, at least in the first decades of its existence. Also undeniably important was the role of Russian, through the help of which millions of people of over 130 nationalities attained their education, had their first encounter with cultures of the world, got to know better the diverse and complementary cultures of different people living in the Soviet Union. The cultural and spiritual aspirations of people grew faster than anything else. The higher those aspirations were, the more people understood the discrepancies of the rigid bureaucratic apparatus, which was fossilizing daily and trying to isolate people from the flow of information.

It is irrelevant to argue whether the metropoly or the peripheral regions fared better. But, united under a single umbrella, over 130 nations and ethnic groups needed a common means of communication in order to coexist and interact. Such means of communication was provided by the Russian language.

The unitary nature of the Soviet Union determined the role of the Russian language: a centralized economy, a uniform system of education to serve its needs, a powerful military establishment all were logically based primarily on the Russian language. In economic terms, this orientation ensured a very high mobility of manpower. In education, the common Russian language allowed people of various ethnic origins to seek and find employment in government agencies as well as to be able to move and be moved throughout the country. Communication among central, republican, and regional authorities was carried out in Russian. It was only natural that the powerful armed forces should have communicated in Russian, the one most-spoken and most-known language.

As a matter of declared policy, the Russian language was the means of inter-ethnic communication.[1] Officially, it did not enjoy any preference.[2] But in practice, it became dominant, not in the least through the efforts of some local officials who tried to acquire extra favors from the central government in Moscow.

On the other hand, for millions of people of different nationalities, the Russian language was the tool to get acquainted with civilizations of the world. The number of translations of literary, cultural, and scientific publications from Arabic, Chinese, English, French, German, Hindi, Japanese, Spanish, and dozens of other languages into Russian was the highest in the world. It is clear that to do this the volume of translations into all 130 languages of the Soviet Union would be neither practical nor financially possible. It is also true that most original publications in those 130 languages were translated into Russian and thus became accessible to all readers in the Soviet Union.

To be more personal and specific, for me as a Russian, who grew up and was educated in Moscow, Russian cultural heritage has always included the names of T. Shevchenko, V. Latsis, S. Rustavelli, Churlionis, Aitmatov, Rytcheu, J. Kupala, and dozens of other names of writers, artists, and poets from various parts of the former Soviet Union who are part of our educational background. The dominating role of Russian in the Soviet Union was, thus, unavoidable. This role is now a part of the past. In a way, that may be good.

Many books were written on the subject of the historic role of the Russian people: whether as a barrier between East and West or as a conductor of cultural experiences. The Russians are occasionally called the people of seven winds, open to influences from all sides. Accordingly, the Russian language has continued to develop over hundreds of years, open to contributions by all the peoples who came in contact with the Russian people. This contact only enriched the language; it became more versatile and universal. I believe the language has a life of its own and to relate it to this or that sociopolitical event does not seem appropriate. In this respect, the Russian language itself has nothing to do with the post-Cold-War era. The language itself has not lost anything yet. On the contrary, it gains in the process. We can speak only of role changes and resultant problems for people.

In many parts of the former Soviet Union, such changes and problems are quite profound. We witnessed first how states of Eastern Europe went through transformations. Then, genuine changes took place within the Soviet Union itself. Historians now have a subject to play with for many years to come: who won the Cold War? For the purpose of this essay, it is important to note that first announcements regarding the end of the Cold War were made in Russian.

As a result of these changes, there are fifteen independent sovereign states where there used to be a unitary state. The 130 nationalities of that state are scattered about these fifteen states, and dozens of millions of people are confronted with language problems. In practically all these new states new laws have been adopted, among them laws proclaiming native languages as the languages of official usage. As the former language of inter-ethnic communication of 130 nationalities, Russian, in effect a second native language for a great majority of people, was moved to the backstage of political and social life, although safeguarded in a few states as the language of Russian minorities.

The situation of minorities has been a long-standing concern for the United Nations. Article 1 of its Charter provides for international cooperation in "promoting and encouraging respect for human rights and for fundamental freedoms for all without distinction as to race, sex, *language* [emphasis added], or religion." But we cannot say that international cooperation for this purpose has reached all the minorities in all the newly independent states that were part of the former Soviet Union. One may argue that the imposition, by the previous regime, of Russian throughout the Soviet Union was wrong. But in a democratic society, one wrong should not be redressed by another.

There is no denying that people living in a given cultural and ethnic environment need to learn the customs and cultural heritage of that environment, including, first of all, the native language. True, many Russians living outside Russia proper failed, or did not want, to do so. But to demand that millions should write and speak native languages overnight, without giving them time or providing suitable infrastructure (schools, courses, books, etc.) amounts to a set of practices with implications that could hardly be called appropriate in a democracy.

Many parts of the former Soviet Union (and I have personally traveled across most of it) are now engulfed by the flames of nationalistic emotions. As a language professional, in many instances, I see the repetition of mistakes made by some Communist bosses who, through insufficient educational or cultural background treated languages without respect, not understanding the delicate nature of this most important feature of human experience and cultural tradition.

In an age of change, nothing is riskier than a sure thing. Betting that things will continue on their present course is high-risk behavior. Trends create countertrends. Nothing is forever, except human experience, reflected in languages. At this point, is it appropriate to ask whether the language formerly used as an official and working language on one sixth of the world's territory has lost the right to be called one of the six official working languages of the United Nations? We have the answer, and it is: no. Russian was confirmed as an official and working language in the statement by the representative of the Russian Federation in the Fifth Committee, after consultations and concurrence by member states of the Commonwealth of Independent States (CIS).

From a strictly quantitative point of view, there is currently only one state on the globe using Russian as its official language: the Russian Federation (without mentioning several members of the CIS that mention Russian in their new constitutions). The other former users of Russian have switched—or at least tried to switch—to other working languages of the United Nations, mostly to English. But is it possible to make such a switch overnight?

We could hardly exaggerate in saying that as of today few of the former Soviet republics are able to process the huge flow of UN documentation in any other official and working language of the UN but Russian. As an example, not long ago we had to deal with an urgent request from the Statistical Office of the UN to translate into Russian a huge volume of statistical questionnaires to be sent to national statistical offices in the capitals of member states of the CIS, previously sent in English to the Central Statistical Office in Moscow. Of secondary but illustrative significance, the Russian edition of the *UN Journal*, which in Soviet times was readily available on the ground floor of the Secretariat, is now hard to find because the number of users—measured in delegations, not individuals—has increased from three to fifteen.

As soon as the last vestiges of Russian supremacy—including linguistic aspects of this phenomenon—are eliminated, the Russian language, maybe for the first time in its history, will truly become a universal tool of inter-state, international communication. It will facilitate normalization of economic, trade, and financial relations between member states of the CIS, and between old partners in Eastern Europe and CIS members. There is a sharp growth in demand everywhere for professionals with practical knowledge of Russian. It is hard to imagine that any company wishing to conduct business on the territory of the former Soviet Union would take along 100 interpreters for the different languages encountered there.

The Russian Federation has already drawn some practical lessons from linguistic changes in the CIS. Training of interpreters and translators to work with member states of the CIS has started at the former

Moscow Institute of Foreign Languages, now called the Moscow Linguistic University. For many years, the Russian language will serve as an intermediary between 130 nationalities and the rest of the world, unless leaders of some newly independent states or autonomous regions would wish an economic, cultural, and spiritual autarky for their people. Russian is now and will always be at the disposal of the world community as one of the great languages of the world, as part of human heritage, always ready for good service to all those who do know how to use it but (we hope temporarily) try to pretend they do not.

Notes

[1] According to the 1979 census data 93.1% of the populace considered the language of their nationality as their mother tongue; 6.9% chose other languages. 214.8 million (82%) considered Russian as their mother tongue or second native language (6.3 million compared with 41.9 million in 1970).

[2] Constitution of the USSR. See, for example, article 34,
> Citizens of the USSR are equal before the law, without distinction of origin, social or property status, race or nationality, sex, education, language, attitude to religion, type and nature of occupation, domicile, or other status

article 36,
> Citizens of the USSR of different races and nationalities have equal rights. Exercise of these rights is ensured by ... the possibility to use their native language and the languages of other peoples of the USSR

article 45,
> ... the right to education.... is ensured by ... the opportunity to attend a school where teaching is in the native language

article 116,
> Laws of the USSR and decisions and other acts of the Supreme Soviet of the USSR shall be published in the languages of the Union Republics

and article 159
> Judicial proceedings shall be conducted in the language of the Union Republic, Autonomous Republic, Autonomous Region, or Autonomous Area, or in the language spoken by the majority of the people in the locality. Persons participating in court proceedings, who do not know the language in which they are being conducted, shall be ensured the right to become fully acquainted with the materials in the case; the services of an interpreter during the proceedings; and the right to address the court in their own language.

The Perestroika of the Russian Language: From Marx to Marketing

Lynn Visson

In a December 1992 issue of *Time*, the Moscow bureau chief, John Kohan, referred to Gogol's image of Russia in the 19th century as a

> wildly careening troika rushing off into the unknown. Some passengers are worried that there will be a colossal breakdown en route. Others are experiencing motion sicknessss as they try to grapple with new ideas like demokratizatsiya and privatizatsiya or attempt to figure out what makes brokery different from raketeery.[1]

For centuries Russia has been torn between two opposing trends: should she turn for inspiration to the West, and borrow Western words and concepts, forms of government, literature, and art, or should she look into the mirror of her own Slavic culture, based on Slavic linguistic roots, Russian Orthodoxy, Russian folklore, Russian literature and art? The conflict between the so-called Slavophiles and Westernizers predates even the era of Peter the Great's reforms, which opened Russia to the West, and stirred up heated linguistic and patriotic passions. Even the briefest gallop through the history of the Russian language will show how acute this conflict has always been—and continues to be.

From the very beginning, Russian was subjected to strong foreign influences. In the ninth century, Old Church Slavonic, which was based on a Bulgarian dialect from the area around Salonika, became the literary language of Russia. It was stuffed with Greek words and modeled on Greek syntax. From the start, too, the language used in Russia was divided into strictly differentiated stylistic levels. The Church used undiluted Old Church Slavonic; the administrative, bureaucratic language of Russian officialdom differed from the Church language and also from the spoken language (in fact, in terms of its artificial vocabulary, odd turns of phrase and distorted grammar, I think the administrative language strongly resembles that used in the United Nations). And I will argue that in Russia the distinction between the written and spoken language throughout the nation's history has been greater than in many other countries, possibly the result of centuries of a dictatorial bureaucratic system which used the iron grip of stultified language to impose its will on the nation from top to bottom and from corner to corner. That written bureaucratic language became even more frozen during the some 200 years of the 13–15th centuries when Russia was cut off from the world by the Mongol invasion (which, incidentally, left behind such words as деньги [den'gi] (money) or кумыс [kumys] (sour milk).

Russian in the 17th century was filled with Slavonic calques from Greek, the original language of the Orthodox Church: e.g., богоносец [bogonosec] (Godbearer, from the Greek theotokos or звездозаконие [zvezdozakonie] (from Greek *astronomia*). There were also many words directly borrowed from Greek, such as ангел [angel], икона [ikona], or епископ [episkop]. There were also very long Greek-Slavonic combined words, such as разумоподательный [razumopodatel'nyj] (that which is subject to reason) or разнопестровидный [raznopestrovidnyj] (something in varied bright colors).

The secular age of Peter the Great tended to discard Slavonic roots and words. The literary language was now Russian, not Church Slavonic. But, as one scholar has written, "it was a curious Russian, full of Slavonic reminiscences and saturated with undigested words of every conceivable foreign origin—Greek, Latin, Polish, German, Dutch, Italian, and French."[2] The newly modified alphabet introduced Slavonic letters adapted to resemble Latin ones (some were derived from Hebrew and Greek). Peter's ukazes called for the study of foreign languages and for the translation of a huge number of foreign works into Russian. His interest in how military matters and engineering were treated abroad soon expanded to almost all areas of life. As one writer noted,

> The Russians started with foreign soldiers and German cannon and ended with the German ballet and Latin grammar. ... Dutch sea captains, French military engineers and German artillerists, all greatly favored by Peter, were followed by Leibniz, Diderot, and Lessing.[3]

Under Peter the Great, the Russian language acquired hundreds of foreign terms, many from science, medicine, and the military arts: нумерация [numeraciia], глобус [globus], минута [minuta], дистанция [distanciia], or фундамент [fundament]. The borrowings spread to other fields as well, e.g., words such as публикация [publikaciia], персона [persona]. One study showed that about ¼ of the foreign words in Russian in the Petrine era dealt with administrative matters, e.g., губернатор [gubernator], министр [ministr], сенат [senat], ордер [order].[4] Slowly other areas of European manners and civilization also crept into the language: деликатный [delikatnyj], фамилиарный [familiarnyj], пассаж [passazh], рекомендовать [rekomendovat'].

By the 18th century some writers were complaining that no one could understand Slavonic any more. One complained that "язык славенский жесток моим ушам слышится" [iazyk slavenskij zhestok moim usham slyshitsia] (The Slavonic language is harsh to my ears).[5] The Russian Benjamin Franklin, Mikhail Lomonosov, the scientist, poet, scholar, and linguist who founded Moscow University in 1755 (and for whom it is named) divided Russian into three styles, high, middle, and low, with the high style distinguished by an abundance of Slavonic elements, the middle style being the written Russian official and literary language, and the low style the colloquial, spoken language. This strict style division has continued from the Middle Ages down into the 20th century.

Lomonosov tried to get rid of Germanic-Latin syntax and introduce a more fluid, French-influenced style. By the end of the 18th and into the early 19th century, the founder of Russian sentimentalism, Nikolai Karamzin, was introducing French calques reflecting the new sensibility: симпатия [simpatiia], меланхолия [melanxoliia], гармония [garmoniia], and such clear Gallic borrowings as принять решение [priniat' reshenie] (take a decision), сломать лед [slomat' led] (break the ice), and не в своей тарелке [ne v svoej tarelke] (feel ill at ease [cf. Fr. n'être pas dans son assiette]). The gap between the written and spoken language began to merge into the "middle style," but patriotic passions were running high. "Glory to thee, O Russian tongue," proclaimed the champion of "pure," Slavic-rooted Russian, Alexander Shishkov, "for thou dost not possess that vile and foul word—Revolution!" Foreign words and style were seen as reflections of the evil influence of French republicanism.[6] Russia has always been torn between a deep-rooted feeling that what is natively Russian is by definition best, and that whatever is foreign must be imitated, adopted, and is better. This contradictory, combined inferiority-superiority complex is succinctly expressed in an old Soviet joke about the schoolteacher who asks a student to list the problems in capitalist America. "Discrimination, poverty, slums, unemployment and hunger," answers the child. "Very good, dear," says the teacher. "And what is our goal in the socialist USSR?" "To catch up with and surpass America, comrade teacher," replies the student. So, too, in linguistics, for many Russians, Russian-Slavic roots were best—but foreignisms were to be admired and adopted.

The height of the adoption of foreign words took place in the reign of Alexander I in the early 19th century, when French essentially replaced Russian as the language of the aristocracy and educated classes. Most of these Russians knew French as well as or better than Russian; the great Russian writer Pushkin said that it was easier for him to express himself in French than in Russian when he had anything to say in prose that was not merely descriptive of fact.[7] And one of the greatest—if not the greatest—novels of Russian literature, *War and Peace*, begins in French, not in Russian.

With Soviet power, the language, too, underwent a revolution. The literary language of the upper classes was to be abolished; a unique Soviet idiom was to be created from the language of workers and peasants. Under Stalin, foreign words were taboo, a sign of bourgeois or rootless cosmopolitan leanings. The language became riddled with bureaucratic clichés, ponderous sentences with enormous subordinate clauses, lengthy acronyms, e.g., mash-pro-sel-torg-etc, and an entirely new political jargon was born which pervaded all aspects of language and life. During the thaw in 1953 one critic complained that even in works about love, the characters talked as if they were making speeches at a public meeting.[8] For that period, clearly, the "Slavophiles" had won out.

Soviet literature on stylistics stressed the importance of "functional styles": the "scientific style" (научный [nauchnyj]), journalistic (публицистический [publicisticheskij]), literary, and colloquial styles, with a rigidity that made these styles look very similar to the Church Slavonic of medieval documents or the bombastic official-administrative style of the 17th century. In fact, the rigidity of Marxist jargon made it a worthy successor to its iron-clad Church Slavonic ancestor. For decades the entire country expressed itself in Marxist clichés, convoluted sentences, and ideas which never came directly to the point. The jargon was a way of keeping safe. Everyone used it for all subjects.

A change or addition of a single phrase could be momentous. When Gorbachev used the innocent-sounding phrase "universal human values," stating that these were higher than the interest of any class, millions of orthodox Marxists jumped; that meant the class conflict and revolution were no longer the bases for social and political life. Phrases in the jargon acquired meanings of their own which everyone knew: "Всем известно, что" [Vsem izvestno, chto] (Everyone knows that ...) was most often followed by something no one had ever heard of. The same held true for "Всем известный" [Vsem izvestnyj] (A person known to all), often used for some alleged enemy of the Soviet state who was also utterly unknown to anyone except the author of the article. A "дружеский открытый разговор" [druzheskij, otkrytyj razgovor] (friendly, open conversation) at negotiations meant that the parties had probably torn each other to pieces. "Есть мнение, что" [Est' mnenie, chto] (There is an opinion that), from a boss to a subordinate, followed by something such as "You should be transferred to Siberia" meant that the question had irrevocably been decided at the top with no hope of appeal. "не надо" [Ne nado] (One shouldn't, there is no need to) do or say something could be heavily politically charged—e.g., you shouldn't do that, and if you do you are in great danger of getting a reprimand, being fired, or whatever.

Writers, journalists, and ordinary people in their daily speech habits engaged in self-censorship in addition to following the rules of official censorship, and an entire Aesopian language grew up to express things one could not say officially. Someone who was "наш" [nash] or "свой человек" [svoi chelovek] was one of the good guys, with us against "them," "they" being the authorities, the government, or the KGB. Now, with the collapse of the old Communist system, the breakdown of Marxist jargon has been accompanied by a collapse of the old way of thinking. At this stage, however, it is open season on linguistic confusion. Some of the old clichés have taken back their original meaning. A "friendly, open conversation" now may be exactly that—unless the author is still thinking old style. It is not so easy overnight to drop all of the old clichés, verbal smokescreens, and habits and suddenly speak and write openly, bluntly, and directly. One newspaper correspondent complained that now he hated writing a weekly column. In the past, he had been able to put one interesting idea into his article and bury it under a mountain of Marxist jargon, forcing the reader to dig out this brilliant nugget by reading between the lines. Now the readers expected a dozen interesting ideas expressed in clear prose in a single such article, and the journalist complained that he simply didn't have so many interesting ideas! The removal of official and self-censorship has created a lexical and stylistic free-for-all which will need several years to even out into a layer of literary language. One result already, however, is a vast narrowing of the enormous gap which existed between the written and spoken language during the pre-perestroika period.

A major development of post-perestroika Russian usage has been the introduction of a huge number of foreign terms, particularly in the fields of business and technology. Not surprisingly, most of these come from English, the international language of these fields. Here Russian is faced with the old Slavophile-Westernizer conflict. Will the word for "marketing" be "исследование рынка" [issledovanie rynka] (research on the market) or "маркетинг" [marketing]? Вычислительная [Vychislitel'naja], машина [mashina], or компьютер [komputer]? The anglicisms have won out, just as the 17th-century звездозаконие [zvezdozakonie] was replaced by астрономия [astronomiia]. (By the way, the anglicisms didn't always win: увраж [uvrazh] (work, as in a work of art) lost to the Slavic root произведение [proizvedenie], and десператный [desperatnyj] lost to отчаянный [otchaiannyj]). But in science and technology, the anglicisms tended to prevail.

I would like to digress for a moment from Russian and point out a parallel with another language which was also forced to choose between its own roots and English ones for modern, scientific, and technical terminology since it did not have most of these words in its lexicon. This is modern Hebrew, and its development shows interesting parallels to the Slavophile–Westernizer controversy. While

Russia was cut off from the West for several centuries and missed out on whole layers of lexical data, Hebrew emerged as a modern language in an Israel quite different from the land of the Bible. Abraham and Moses did not have to work with telephones or psychologists. The Israeli counterparts to Russia's Slavophiles wanted to use Hebrew roots; the Westernizers, English ones. *Psikhòlogia* won out over the Hebrew roots *bri'iut hanefesh*, but this term is still used to mean mental health. *Sotsiologiia* and *sigaria* won over Hebrew roots. But the telephone is a *sakh rakkhot* [to speak at a distance], not *telefon*.[9]

A digression from a digression: Chinese, too, was faced with the task of creating an entirely new scientific and technical vocabulary. Yet because it is a pictorial language in which each syllable must be represented by a written character, such mass borrowings from English are unthinkable, as they would lead to the creation of nonsense syllables and words. China, too, as its political system became rigidly Marxist, rejected as bourgeois influence any hint of foreign borrowing. It is interesting though, that in post-war Japan, Japanese, which has a phonetic alphabet in addition to kanji, has swallowed up an enormous number of English words—the well-known *beisubolu* (baseball) and *taipuraita* (typewriter) to give just two examples. An extremely interesting study could be done on the extent to which various modern languages today have borrowed foreign scientific, technical, business, and other terminology from English or other Western languages, or chosen to create lexical items based on their own roots. The relationship between these patterns of choice and questions of national identity and political systems would be most intriguing.

Back to Russian: Under Stalin, foreignisms were very *mal vu*, and well into the 1960s and '70s, new English words made their way into Russian primarily as very technical terms or through the language of the youth, drug, or hippie subcultures and countercultures. Use of such anglicisms were a sign of protest against the regime: e.g., the hippies' use of words such as батл [batl], герла [gerla], драгсы [dragsy], дринк [drink], клоуз [klouz], олды [oldy] (parents) френд [frend], крейзовать [krejzovat'] (to get very upset). The youth pop culture of rock and roll also made a dent on Russian, e.g., рокеры [rokery] with their джинсы [dzhinsy], and металлисты [metallisty] (heavy metal). The Slavophile linguistic counterculture was that of camp slang, which reached its heyday in the '60s and '70s, and was almost entirely based on Russian roots.

While the 19th century borrowings from French came mostly from the intelligentsia and were transmitted through the aristocracy, these English borrowings of the '60s and '70s came through and to much lower-placed social strata. English began to move from protest subcultures into other fields such as sports— финишировать [finishirovat'] or лидировать [lidirovat'], which then moved out of sports and into normal language. In the area of banking, finance, and—above all—technology, Russian had quickly to acquire an enormous vocabulary. Here Russians were faced with a problem similar to that of Russian émigrés in America. For some "new" concepts, words in fact did exist in Russian: e.g., попечитель [popechitel'] for a sponsor, вклад [vklad] for investment, or ипотека [ipoteka] for mortgage. But many of these terms were very rarely used or sounded archaic or купеческий [kupecheskij], reminiscent of the merchant class. Emigrés quickly tend to start talking about мортгейдж [mortgejdzh] rather than using ипотека [ipoteka]. Попечитель [Popechitel'] was replaced by the Russian спонсор [sponsor], вклад [vklad] by инвестиция [investiciia]. By now, nearly the entire Russian computer terminology comes from English; the early ЭВМ—электронно-вычислительная машина [elektronnovychislitel'naja mashina] was long ago displaced by компьютер [komputer]. Принтер [printer], байты [bajty], and он-лайн [on-lajn] are part of the Russian language. A financial dictionary essentially gives transliterations followed by explanations of the term, e.g., "Broker-dealer : брокер-дилер, company which combines functions of a broker (intermediary) and dealer (principal) participants in leading securities markets (US., Japan, UK) who have the right to be both brokers and dealers)."[10] Or: "Debit spread: дебитовый спред, difference in cost of two options (опционов) when the cost of one bought is higher than the cost of the one sold."[11]

One reason this new technical vocabulary has so quickly been absorbed into Russian is because of the language's ability to add prefixes and suffixes around a root and to make various forms of nouns including diminutives—send a факсик [faksik] (a little fax), or ксероксировать [kseroksirovat'] to make a xerox.[12] And these business-technological borrowings are purely pragmatic; they are neither "aristocratic," as were the French borrowings of the 19th century, or the protest of subcultures, as was the case with the anglicisms of the hippy-drug culture of the '70s.

Critics of such widespread adoption of anglicisms have remonstrated, as one did in a letter to *Literaturnaya gazeta*, that "this is an absence of taste; many simplistically link 'unswerving progress' with a foreign source, rejecting, often unconsciously, their own 'wretched and powerless' homeland."[13] But the trend to take over the ready-made computer-business language seems unstoppable.

Today modern Russian is very much in flux. With the breakdown of the old Marxist jargon, the rigid system of styles, governmental and self-imposed censorship, Aesopian language, the narrowing of the gap between the written and spoken language, and with the onslaught of foreignisms, the Russian seen in today's newspapers and magazines and the spoken language heard on the streets would have been unthinkable a decade ago. Stylistic categories have broken down, grammar and spelling are up for grabs, new terms are invented daily, and vulgarisms abound. Curse words which were never used publicly now can be widely heard. I would argue that one major reason for these new developments is the overwhelming influence of television, with its use of spoken and colloquial language, and that with the breakdown of rigid controls this spoken language of TV now has also started to dominate the print media. Mediatization of speech is leading to a breakdown in youth speech patterns much as in the US; there is far more "это самое, эта штука, вы знаете" [eto samoe, eta shtuka, vy znaete] than there was previously ("that, uh, thing there, like, you know what I mean"). And when needed, the influence of foreign cultures can be blamed for this breakdown. To return to John Kohan at *Time*:

> Judging from Cyrillic-lettered Coca-Cola signs and Barbie doll billboards in Moscow these days, the Westernizers seem to have the upper hand in their century-long debate with the Slavophiles. But, as one Slavic scholar, James Billington, has pointed out, "Repeatedly, Russians have sought to acquire the end products of other civilizations without the intervening process of slow growth and inner understanding... Every time a slapdash imitation of something Western goes wrong, the Slavophiles latch on to it as evidence of the danger posed by alien ideas."[14]

Will the pendulum swing back to the Slavophiles? In a global village linked by telecommunications, international business, and computers, in a world Russia is trying desperately hard to join, that seems most unlikely. But only time can tell how the language and culture will ultimately develop, whether the switch from Marx to marketing has been made once and forever.

Notes

[1] John Kohan, "A Mind of Their Own," *Time*, 7 December 1992, 66.
[2] D.S. Mirsky, *A History of Russian Literature from its Beginnings to 1900* (New York: Vintage Books, 1958), 34.
[3] Marc Slonim, *The Epic of Russian Literature: From its Beginnings through Tolstoy* (New York: Oxford UP, 1964), 21–22.
[4] V. D. Levin, *Краткий очерк истории русского литературного языка* (Москва: Учпедгиз, 1958), 90.
[5] Ibid., 102.
[6] Slonim, 53.
[7] Mirsky, 118.
[8] Marc Slonim, *Soviet Russian Literature* (New York: Oxford UP, 1967), 294.
[9] I am grateful to my colleague Sandra Meron of the United Nations Interpretation Service for the Hebrew examples.
[10] B. G. Fedorov, *Англо-русский толковый словарь валютно-кредитных терминов* (Москва: Финансы и статистика, 1992), 29.
[11] Ibid., 11.
[12] See Serge Schmemann, "Russia Talks Business," *The New York Times Magazine*, 18 October 1992.
[13] Ibid.
[14] *Time*, 7 December 1992, 69.

The Contribution of Language Planning and Language Policy to the Reconciliation of Unity and Diversity in the Post-Cold-War Era

Timothy Reagan

> Concerns about ethnic relations are ubiquitous today. They engage all sorts of countries—Western and non-Western, large and small, democratic and nondemocratic, rich and poor—even those with no ethnic minorities. Since the early 1960s, troublesome issues centered on ethnocultural distinctions have arisen in many modern societies in the West, once considered free of—or no longer susceptible to—politically significant ethnicity. And the presence of large numbers of migrants and refugees has added multiethnic dimensions to previously homogeneous societies. (Heisler, 1990, p. 21)

Heisler's observations about the ubiquity of ethnicity in the contemporary world are, if anything, even more true today than when he offered them in 1990. One of the consequences of the break-up of the Soviet Union, and of several formerly unified states in eastern Europe, has been a significant rise in the visibility of both ethnicity and nationalism as important social, political, and economic forces. Underlying the tensions that this resurgence of ethnicity and nationalism has brought about has been an inevitable tension between pluralistic pressures for identity and self-government on the part of both small and large groups on the one hand, and pressures for national unity and unification on the other. Closely paralleling the growing power of ethnic and national identity has also been the rise of the historic demons of xenophobia, anti-Semitism, and racism in many places. We see these tensions in the process of resolution not only in parts of the former Soviet Union, but also in Czechoslovakia, the parts of the former Yugoslavia, and, manifested in different ways, in the reunited Germany. Indeed, there are few parts of Europe (or in the rest of the world, for that matter) where the effects of this ethnic and nationalist resurgence have not been felt. Ethnicity, which until quite recently was a concern primarily of those in the developing world, has, in short, reappeared on the doorstep, and even in the living room, of the developed world with a vengeance.

Ethnicity and ethnic identity are vast and complex topics, of course, and deserve far more attention than could possibly be provided here (see, e.g., Glazer and Moynihan, 1975; Lijphart, 1977; Young, 1976). Rather, my focus will be far narrower—I want to briefly address the role that can be played by language planning and language policy in reconciling the competing pressures for diversity and unity, as well as the limitations on that role, first in general terms, and then with specific focus on Europe.

The Role of Language Planning and Language Policy

In addressing the role that can be played by language planning and language policy activities in contributing to the reconciliation of the forces for diversity and the pressures for unity, one of the most important things for us to understand is that the nature of this struggle—and a struggle it all too often is—is one that almost always goes far beyond language, language differences, and language rights (see Fishman, 1989; Tollefson, 1991). Language is a powerful symbol of ethnic and national identity, to be sure, and the selection of a national or official language has both symbolic and practical consequences (Cooper, 1989). Language often serves as a focal point for calls for ethnic and national rights, and the idea that language is somehow a necessary condition of ethnic identity remains common. This linkage between language and group identity is central in understanding the power of language issues in ethnic conflicts. This linkage of language to other aspects of ethnic and national conflict is one with extensive historical roots. Many nationalists today would agree with Cicero's sentiment, "The language of the conqueror in the mouth of the conquered is the language of slaves."

And yet, having recognized the importance of language, it is also clear that significant ethnic differences can exist in the absence of major language differences (as the case of the Serbians and the Croatians makes clear), just as the presence of language difference does not inevitably mean ethnic conflict. Language is one, admittedly important, aspect of diversity, but others—historical differences, religious differences, economic differences, political differences, cultural differences, geographic differences, and so on—often play important roles in national and ethnic divisions as well.

What all this means for language planners and policy-makers is quite simple: language planning and language policy activities may have important emotive, psychological, and symbolic value, but they cannot, on their own, resolve other, arguably more important, differences between and among ethnic and national groups. No language policy will end the fighting in Bosnia (see Bugarski and Hawkesworth, 1992), nor would any language policy solve the problems faced by Germans and "guestworkers" as they try to live together (see Nelde et al., 1981). With a few notable exceptions, on their own language policy and language planning are unlikely to play a central role in resolving the tension between pressures for diversity and pressures for unity.

However, it is also important to note that while language planning and language policy activities may not be able to contribute positively to such a reconciliation in a central way, they can most certainly have a powerful impact in the other direction. That is, language policies can, and do, make matters worse, and this, I would suggest, is the real challenge for those involved in language planning and language policy endeavors. Because language is a highly charged emotional component of ethnic and national identity for many groups, slights (whether real or imagined) to the group's language are often taken to be slights of the group itself. Thus, poorly conceived language policies have resulted in riots and deaths in a number of places around the world, not because of linguistic issues *per se*, but rather, because of what those linguistic issues are taken to represent. For example, the 1976 Soweto uprising in South Africa was initially inspired by students' resistance to a change in educational policy that would have resulted in greater use of Afrikaans, a language seen by many South Africans as the "language of the oppressor," although the issues underlying the uprising obviously had more to do with political and economic facets of apartheid rather than with the language policy at stake (see Reagan, 1987). The role of ideology in this process, incidentally, cannot be underestimated in terms of its significance and impact (see Joseph and Taylor, 1990; Tollefson, 1991, pp. 22–42).

As we consider possible language policy options, it might be a good idea for us to adopt a standard maxim used by physicians: *primum nihil nocere*. The basic idea with *primum nihil nocere* is that whatever else one does with patients, one ought not make them worse than they were when treatment began. A similar dictum ought to apply to those involved in language planning and language policy activities: whatever else we do, we shouldn't exacerbate problems, nor should we contribute to things that make ethnic and national tensions worse than they were when we started. Although easy to agree to in principle, this dictum is often difficult to apply in practice, since it is not always clear what will make things worse and what will make them better.

With the goal of trying to practice *primum nihil nocere* in mind, let us turn now to the case of Europe in the post-Cold War era.

The Case of the "New" Europe

Both in ethnic and linguistic terms, Europe is highly diverse, and the effects of this diversity are already making themselves felt throughout the continent. With respect to linguistic diversity, both in the European Community (EC) and on the continent writ large, language differences will continue to constitute important challenges for inter-national and intra-national organizations and government bodies for the foreseeable future. Language policies and language planning activities will be significant components and targets of government, business, and EC policy, of this there can be little doubt; what remains are questions about what types of language policies and language planning activities are most likely to be undertaken, and what kinds of options should be considered.

The range of language policy and language planning options open to Europe can actually be envisaged as following along a "continuum of diversity," ranging from the most pluralistic to the most unified. At one extreme of this continuum, all languages used on the continent would be accorded equal status and rights, regardless of their number of speakers, level of development in terms of technical terminology, and so on. Such an option, although certainly tolerant and pluralistic, is obviously unworkable, for practical and economic reasons if for no others. At the opposite end of the continuum, a single language would be used and would have official status throughout the continent. Again, such an option would obviously be unacceptable—no existing European nation state is likely to agree to abandon its language, nor, even should a government agree to such a proposition, would the population at large comply. Realistic language policy options for Europe will obviously fall somewhere between these two extremes, and will have to address a plethora of issues related to matters of equity, fairness, utility, degree of development, economic viability, and so on. The challenge will be to address these issues in a manner that does not create new and even more troublesome problems—that is, to avoid making the patient worse.

While I suspect that the solution to the challenge of reconciling competing pressures for diversity and unity in Europe will be along the lines already employed in the EC, it does occur to me that such a solution is not really the most reasonable one. Such a solution inevitably requires an immense expenditure in terms of interpreting, translation and publications services, and so on, while at the same time it will in essence favor the existing "languages of wider communication" (such as English and French), and penalize the smaller languages (e.g., Catalan, Danish, and so forth). The use of a single, relatively neutral language—however one chooses to define "neutrality" in this context—in conjunction with continued use of national, regional, and ethnic languages would provide a possible alternative, both internationally and intra-nationally, and might be both cheaper and more effective in the long run. Such a language, as we have often been told in the past at CRD conferences, is, of course, Esperanto.

I want to make clear, though, that in suggesting that Esperanto be seriously considered as a viable and realistic language policy option for Europe (and, in fact, perhaps elsewhere as well), I am not doing so as an Esperantist. I do not speak Esperanto and am not formally affiliated with the Esperanto movement. While, perhaps, for the Esperantists among us, this is not a virtue, it does provide, I would suggest, at least limited evidence of a degree of impartiality. An important characteristic of the Esperanto movement has been its idealism and commitment to a set of social and quasi-religious ideals; while I have no quarrel with these ideals, my concern with Esperanto is based solely on what I take to be its practical benefits, and it is on the basis of those benefits that its possible role in the reconciliation of the competing pressures for diversity and unity in various contexts ought to be considered. This is an important point, given the common view of Esperanto and its movement as "fringe" in nature (see Forster, 1982).

The pragmatic advantages of Esperanto, in a nutshell, are:

1. It is neutral, at least in the sense that it is not a national or ethnic language. This advantage alone is significant, in that the selection of a language medium, for whatever purpose, inevitably implies not selecting some other language or languages. No matter how widely spoken, a language like English or French will always be closely identified with the communities for which they are native languages. Although one may discuss the "Africanization" of English or French, as some African writers have done, the fact remains that these languages are closely identified with their ethnic communities.
2. Esperanto is demonstrably easier to learn than so-called "natural" languages. It is no secret that some languages are, for a host of reasons, easier to learn than others for speakers of various languages. As Mark Twain wrote in his essay on "The Awful German Language":

    > My philological studies have satisfied me that a gifted person ought to learn English (barring spelling and pronouncing), in thirty hours, French in thirty days, and German in thirty years. (Blair, 1962, p. 192)

    Twain was not alone in his problems with German, incidentally. Thomas Love Peacock, for instance, commented that, "Life is too short to learn German" (Muir, 1976, p. 86), while Heinrich Heine, making a similar point, argued that, "The Romans would never have had time to conquer the world if they had been obliged to learn Latin first of all" (Muir, 1976, p. 60). The point here is a simple one: language learning is a difficult and taxing process, and with Esperanto, one gains an advantage with less time and effort than is needed for virtually any other language.
3. Esperanto already exists, has an international user population, and has an extensive lexicon suited to contemporary needs.

There are, of course, numerous other advantages of Esperanto often cited by Esperantists, including the rich culture and literature that is conducted through the medium of Esperanto (see Auld, 1988; Janton, 1988; Moya, 1989; Mullarney, 1982; Richardson, 1988). For our purposes here, though, it is enough to suggest that Esperanto has enough practical advantages for us to consider more fully its role in the reconciliation of the competing pressures for diversity and unity in various contexts.

Needless to say, just as there are many arguments in support of Esperanto, so, too, there are many objections. For example, one could certainly argue that the inertia of familiarity with multinational organizations that provide interpreting and translation services would strongly favor the status quo, at least until the costs of such services become prohibitive. Also working against Esperanto is the relatively small professional population already familiar with the language; while Esperanto is indeed easier to learn than other languages, the adoption of Esperanto would require a far larger user population than currently exists. Attitudes toward Esperanto, which are often unfavorable, also present a serious obstacle in this respect, regardless of the rationality or irrationality of such critical views. Nonetheless, Esperanto would appear to offer considerable promise, and certainly giving it more serious consideration than has been done in the past would not seem unreasonable.

Conclusion

Any resolution of the concerns about ethnicity in the contemporary world, quoted from Heisler at the beginning of this paper, must involve those interested in language issues. Language planning and language policy can in some instances contribute in meaningful and valuable ways to the resolution of ethnic tensions. I have suggested here that, for the most part, as we evaluate language policy options and language planning endeavors, we would do well to be guided by the principle of *primum nihil nocere*.

References

Auld, W. *La Fenomeno Esperanto*. Rotterdam: Universala Esperanto-Asocio, 1988.
Blair, W. (Ed.). *Selected Shorter Writings of Mark Twain*. Boston: Houghton Mifflin, 1962.
Bugarski, R., and C. Hawkesworth (Eds.). *Language Planning in Yugoslavia*. Columbus, OH: Slavica, 1992.
Cooper, R. *Language Planning and Social Change*. Cambridge: Cambridge UP, 1989.
Fishman, J. *Language and Ethnicity in Minority Sociolinguistic Perspective*. Clevedon: Multilingual Matters Ltd., 1989.
Forster, P. *The Esperanto Movement*. The Hague: Mouton, 1982.
Glazer, N., and D. Moynihan (Eds.). *Ethnicity: Theory and Experience*. Cambridge, MA: Harvard UP, 1975.
Heisler, M. "Ethnicity and Ethnic Relations in the Modern West." In *Conflict and Peacemaking in Multiethnic Societies* Ed. J. Montville. Lexington, MA: Lexington, 1990. 21–52.
Janton, P. *Esperanto: Lingvo, Literaturo, Movado*. Rotterdam: Universala Esperanto-Asocio, 1988.
Joseph, J, and T. Taylor (Eds.). *Ideologies of Language*. London: Routledge, 1990.
Lijphart, A. *Democracy in Plural Societies: A Comparative Exploration*. New Haven: Yale UP, 1977.
Moya, G. *Esperanto en Prospektivo*. Barcelona: Giordano Moya Escayola, 1989.
Muir, F. (Ed.). *An Irrelevant and Thoroughly Incomplete Social History of Almost Everything*. New York: Stein and Day, 1976.
Mullarney, M. *Esperanto for Hope: A New Way of Learning the Language of Peace*. Dublin: Poolbeg, 1989.
Nelde, P., G. Extra, M. Hartig, and M. de Vriendt (Eds.). *Sprachprobleme bei Gastarbeiterkindern*. Tübingen: Narr, 1981.
Reagan, T. "Ideology and Language Policy in Education: The Case of Afrikaans." In *Afrikaans en Taalpolitiek* Ed. H. Du Plessis and T. Du Plessis. Pretoria: Haum, 1987. 133–39.
Richardson, D. *Esperanto: Learning and Using the International Language*. El Cerrito, CA: Esperanto League for North America, in cooperation with Orcas Publishing, 1988.
Tollefson, J. *Planning Language, Planning Inequality: Language Policy in the Community*. London: Longman, 1991.
Young, C. *The Politics of Cultural Pluralism*. Madison: U of Wisconsin P, 1976.

Language Study and Global Education: Approaches to Development of Language and Communication for Bridge-Building in the Post-Cold-War Era

Helene Zimmer-Loew

Some of the most advanced thinking, discussion, and planning on the interrelationship between language study and global education is currently being conducted under the auspices of the Council of Europe. Founded in May 1949 to achieve greater unity among the European parliamentary democracies, the Council of Europe (CE) is the oldest of the European political institutions. Through a flexible system of cooperation among governments, members of parliament, and experts, the Council seeks to protect and develop human rights and democracy and harmonize the policies of its 27 member states in a wide variety of fields including education, culture, social welfare, health, the environment, local government, and justice and thereby promote the emergence of a genuine European identity. Its headquarters is in Strasbourg, France.

The Council for Cultural Cooperation

The CE's work on education and culture is carried out by its appointed and supported Council for Cultural Cooperation (CDCC), which brings together 36 states that have agreed to the European Cultural Convention.

Among the CDCC's programs is "Language Learning for European Citizenship." This program promotes language learning and teaching on the premise that language provides essential support to all other aspects of international cooperation. Unless all participants in the CE's international programs are able to communicate effectively and directly with each other, there can be little successful cooperation.

The aim of the CDCC's various modern language programs has been to

> make more widely available to all sections of the populations of member countries the means of learning to communicate more effectively with other Europeans through each other's languages. This knowledge should (1) facilitate the free movement of individuals; (2) further understanding between peoples through personal contact; (3) improve the effectiveness of European cooperation; and (4) overcome prejudice and discrimination.[1]

The CDCC's work is aimed at supporting the practical implementation of reforms under way in member states and preparing the partners whose cooperation is needed for effective educational innovation. Meeting the challenges of the internationalization of life in Europe and maintaining the diversity of Europe's linguistic and cultural heritage are parallel goals for the CDCC.[2]

European Citizenship

The European dimension has become a major focus of the Council of Europe. The CE ministers have pointed out that work, study, and leisure in Europe are characterized by mobility, interchange, and communication and that the daily lives of Europeans have taken on "a living European dimension." They recommend that education should increase awareness of the growing unity between the countries and peoples of Europe. It should also foster an understanding of the fact that in many spheres of their lives the European perspective applies and European decisions are necessary.

At the same time, the ministers emphasize that people should not lose sight of their global responsibilities or of their national, regional, and local roots. Programs to foster an awareness of Europe must not promote selfish or Eurocentric attitudes. The CE recommends that education systems encourage young people to see themselves "not only as citizens of their own regions and countries but also as citizens of Europe and of the wider world."[3]

Role of Language Learning

One of the major goals of the CDCC's Intergovernmental Symposium held in Sintra, Portugal, in November 1989, was to exchange information on the state of language learning and European citizenship, to make recommendations on this priority area, and to propose concrete actions to develop these recommendations.

A working group on Citizenship in Europe recommended a campaign directed at the adult public in order to (1) promote a non-school view of learning and teaching foreign languages; (2) develop new pre-service training programs for teachers and new training programs for inservice teachers; (3) study "bridges" (linguistic, verbal, socio-cultural, etc.) to facilitate subsequent access to other languages in the European area; and (4) encourage the development of new working instruments to facilitate self-training.

The CDCC also recommended that research be conducted in each member country which would result in a plan to create European citizenship: awareness, belonging, and identity. The plan proposed the conditions, resources, and instruments for a true "European civic education" by encouraging the sharing of connotations (historical, literary, artistic, etc.) from primary level through the mother tongue and during school and university through at least two foreign languages.[4]

Technology Creating the Global Village

Although one may perceive distances between and among European nations as relatively short, the CDCC planners are depending heavily on new technologies to implement their plans. Two CE programs offer models for crossing borders electronically. In the area of telecommunications, through the CDCC, the CE commissioned a study in 1990 on media education for teacher trainers. The resulting publication is *Media Education for Europe—A Teacher's Guide*.

In addition, the CE has supported distance education. Following the parliamentary assembly's recommendation in 1989 on distance education and the resolution on *The Information Society—A Challenge for Education Policies*, the CDCC commissioned a feasibility study on distance education. On the basis of an interim report and wide consultations with public and private, national, and international institutions and associations involved in distance learning, the education committee of the CDCC concluded that all existing CDCC projects should include a distance learning dimension, wherever appropriate.

There is much to be accomplished in this area beginning with the large scale installation of the basic technology needed and the strengthening and modernizing of the present telecommunications infrastructure. Here learners and teachers can leap across languages and borders, giving individuals a broad choice of topics and media. Reliable, powerful telecommunications systems (telephones, fax machines, telecopiers, teleconferencing with TV, electronic mail) are slowly becoming more available to citizens at their workplace and at home. With the help of electronic mail and other computerized systems, there is a growing international network of schools and universities cooperating on joint studies, preparing students for life and work in a multicultural and multilingual society by setting up a global electronic village. Satellite broadcasts keep citizens current on news in many languages, for example, Germany's *Deutsche Welle* on Eutelsat or Intelsat worldwide.

An effective interactive model for professional development networks such as SERC (Satellite Educational Resources Consortium) in the United States may serve as a model for the work of the CDCC. This 23-state partnership of educators and broadcasters provides quality live interactive education coursework via satellite Through SERC, schools can offer coursework that would otherwise be unavailable, and teachers and staff can continue their training without leaving their campuses. Interactive in this program means using the television studio and telephone communications at the learner's site to communicate with the teacher/facilitator. In the long term, such technology is far less expensive than installing a teacher/facilitator on site or having people travel to a course site.

Assisting the Countries of Eastern Europe

A major current concern of the CE is helping the countries of eastern Europe. They need assistance in their lengthy transition to parliamentary democracy and a market economy. Among the training needs are the skills for those responsible for administering the new democracies: lawyers, judges, politicians, local and regional administrators, and union leaders.

There is a great need for the preparation of new legislation, curricula, textbooks and teaching resources, professional development, and the teaching of western European languages, in particular, English, French, and German. Among the other disciplines in greatest need of rebuilding are history, philosophy, political science, law, economics, and business and management studies.

With the many other demands on their fragile economies and new leaders, the necessary investment in education is difficult if not impossible. A brain drain of qualified staff and researchers from higher education to the private sector or to other countries is also a concern.

The scale and diversity of these needs are so great that they will require a sustained response for several years, and they far exceed the capacity of any single European country or institution.[5] Therefore, the CE has supported several programs to train managers and executives for Europe's new democracies. One helps train managerial staff in central and eastern European countries and constitutes a concerted European response to these countries' need for managerial and executive staff.

Another program established a training network designed to increase employment for young people aged 18–25. This network is based on the idea of the French *compagnonnage* movement, the aim of which was to create a mutual support system among craftsmen within a given trade and to offer an outward-looking form of vocational training. These new European journeymen have to spend 12 months abroad working in their own trade, three to six months in each of three different countries. At the end of this training period they are recognized with a certificate. The objectives of this pilot project are to supplement young peoples' vocational training and improve their language skills through job experience in various European countries; to facilitate their employment on return; to increase their geographical and occupational mobility; and to increase their awareness of a European identity. The CE sponsors vocational training courses each year for the trainers of these young people engaged in the trades.

In addition, the CE supports the social development fund which finances vocational training. This has been an effective means to help the resettlement of populations affected by economic, natural, or political reasons trying to reintegrate them into the world of work. Vocational training centers in the target countries are the result of this program as well.

Conclusion

Europe is moving toward an integrated system of life-long learning, or "recurrent education." In its efforts to meet some of the needs of the citizens fo both Western and Eastern Europe, the CE has developed model programs that use language study, distance learning, and international travel and internships to support this system. As they build their vocational skills and knowledge, the students also gain a global perspective, which will serve them well beyond the fast disappearing borders of a greater Europe.

Notes

[1] Council for Cultural Cooperation, 55th Session, 24–27 January 1989. Draft Programme of Activities of the CDCC for 1989: Proposals for Further Action Regarding Language Learning and Teaching 1.

[2] Ibid. 2.

[3] Maitland Stobart, *The New Europe and Education: the Role of the Council of Europe* (Cherry Hill, New Jersey: AATF-AATG, 1993), 8. Joint Publication of the American Association of Teachers of French and the American Association of Teachers of German.

[4] Report of the Intergovernmental Symposium, Sintra, Portugal, 7–11 November 1989 (Strasbourg: Council of Europe, n.d.) 124–25.

[5] Stobart 11–13.

Global Awareness and Language Learning

Margareta Bowen

John Naisbitt's popular book, *Megatrends*, has drawn attention to the parallel growth of opposite trends, e.g., high tech vs. high touch. The continuous reach of technology into our daily lives is accompanied by a counterbalancing development or revival of human values, drawing individual attention to hobbies like crafts. Anyone who owns a telephone-answering machine will be aware of telling examples. Similarly, we observe the longing for a universal language, be it an artificial language like Esperanto or a natural one like English, alongside the growth of multilingualism in countries which used to see (or portray) themselves as monolingual, as well as in international organizations, where the number of official languages has been growing.

Languages in International Organizations

Originally working with five official languages (Chinese, English, French, Russian, and Spanish), the United Nations added Arabic in 1973; a German translation unit was set up in 1975. The European Community, which started with four official languages, has now reached the impressive number of nine, which means 72 language combinations; once the European Free Trade Association's remaining member countries have been fully integrated, still more languages will have to be used, at least in the major bodies of the organization.

The growing importance of what we now call *minority languages* in the United States demonstrates that they have become essential for cultural identity, whereas in the past languages were linked to political (*civis Romanus sum*) or national identity (e.g., the languages of Central and Eastern Europe). The debate over bilingual education in the United States is but the tip of the iceberg. Basque, Catalan, and Gallego in Spain, Breton and Provençal in France, all make their claims.

As long as there was still a Soviet Union, little news reached the West of pressures for multilingualism within its borders, but with the breakup, citizens of the newly independent republics complain about having been deprived of their language.

Language and Context

The statement that a language is inseparable from its culture is easily accepted, but its implications are not so readily recognized. By culture we mean more than the national or regional idiosyncrasies, allusions to literary texts, slang expressions, or references to history, although all these can hamper crosscultural communication and pose major problems for the translator. World events influence the languages we speak, leading to new concepts and hence to new expressions. Therefore, global awareness has to go along with language knowledge. To illustrate the problem, let me quote from a recent entrance examination at Georgetown University. These examinations are held several times a year to determine candidates' access to a one- or two-year program in translation and interpretation. The Spanish text had the clause " ... *las disposiciones de la Carta de las Naciones Unidas.*" Several candidates rendered it as "... the dispositions of the letter of the United Nations." The backgrounds of our candidates vary, but they all had been admitted to a college, usually a selective one, most have a Bachelor's, and some a graduate degree. Even this small fragment of a Spanish text held two distinct problems for the candidate. The first one, *disposiciones*, if rendered correctly, would have rated a plus point because in the text it would come under the heading of prescriptive terminology. It is an item that a candidate would not be expected to know, since it is taught in an advanced translation course. The second one is a typical example of the link between language knowledge and world knowledge. Undoubtedly, one of the first lessons in anyone's Spanish course would include the word *la carta* (the letter), as in "Let's write a letter to a friend in Spain." But anyone in the candidates' age group would also have heard at some time about the basic document of the United Nations, the Charter. Had this piece of information been forgotten, or did the candidate just fail to associate it with *la Carta de las Naciones Unidas*? In more general terms, would better language knowledge alone have avoided a mistranslation like this one? What other factors influence the performance of young people on translation tests?

Preparedness for Translation

In an effort to find answers to these recurring questions, Georgetown University's Division of Interpretation and Translation undertook a three-year study of the factors involved in our undergraduate students' preparedness for advanced translation studies. The project was facilitated by a Title VI grant from the US Department of Education. Let me stress from the outset that *advanced translation studies* does not refer to translation as a language-teaching approach. Since Robert Lado's influential work, translation is seldom used as a method of language teaching in the United States, although recently there have been some indications of a reversal of the trend. Articles by Andrei Danchev, Francisco Gomes de Matos, Lynn Visson, and Georgeanne Weller seem to point this way. The Georgetown students who participated in this study were in advanced language classes, sometimes literature or conversation classes, and had not manifested a desire to learn how to do professional translations. They came in "cold," so to speak, and were asked to translate a short text on a contemporary subject. The detailed description of the study's strategy and statistical approach can be found in *The Jerome Quarterly* 6.4 (1991), together with a discussion of the influence of gender on student performance.

Other than gender, the factors we entered in the statistics were the students' major, academic class, grade-point average, the language combination chosen, length of time spent abroad, and ethnic background. Age did not warrant a separate question, since all participating students were in the normal range for undergraduates. In the context of global awareness, the information to be isolated from this study are major discipline, study abroad, and ethnic background. The data obtained from the test population were analyzed in two ways: (1) trends observed on the basis of the individual test results and (2) trends observed when these results were adjusted according to stratification criteria to form a composite projection of the undergraduate population.

The students who participated in the study were enrolled in

Georgetown University's College of Arts and Sciences, the School of Languages and Linguistics, or the School of Foreign Service. The medical and nursing schools were not included in the project, as proficiency in a foreign language is not required in these programs. A small number of students from the business school were represented in the language classes tested. Data were collected over the three-year period from 1988 to 1991.

The sample consisted of 129 students drawn from the university's upper-level language classes. A class was considered upper-level for the purpose of the study if it was at or beyond the level of "advanced" in Georgetown's progression of foreign language studies (i.e., basic, intermediate, advanced, composition and style, and literature courses). Classes were chosen through incidental sampling, and the stratified-random sampling procedure was to correct anticipated deviations from the composition of the university's student population by weighting individual results in the sample by the percentage of individuals in the university community having similar backgrounds.

The basis for judging results on the examination was the participants' readiness to pursue advanced translation coursework. It should be noted that an entrance examination of this type is required for anyone wishing to register for an advanced translation course because students under the minimum level would not benefit from the course and may hamper the progress of those who qualify. The evaluation included the following three considerations: (1) understanding the message in the source language, (2) ability to express the message clearly and on the appropriate level of style in the target language, and (3) ability to render the original meaning without addition, loss, or distortion. Results were recorded as acceptable, unacceptable, and probationary. An "acceptable" rating indicates that the student is likely to succeed on the university's certification examination at the end of a two-semester course of study. "Probationary" indicates that the results were borderline, and that the student would have to work especially hard to reach the goal by the end of two semesters. "Unacceptable" students are not ready for advanced translation coursework at this stage of their development. For the purposes of the study, the term "successful" has been used for those who demonstrated readiness for advanced translation studies, with or without reservations, i.e., participants who were evaluated as either acceptable or probationary. A "successful" rating should not be taken as an indication that the participant was ready to take on professional assignments as a translator.

The Language Major as a Factor

A thorough understanding of the source language is undoubtedly the most apparent criterion for becoming a translator. Therefore, aspiring translators often feel that they must major in a language. Moreover, some employers stipulate as an educational requirement for positions involving translation that candidates have a major in a language. But there is no unanimity among practicing professionals and educators in the field as to which backgrounds best prepare candidates for the profession. On the one hand, language skills are without doubt a *sine qua non* for a profession that uses language as its main tool. On the other hand, the interpreter and translator must have or be able to readily acquire a sufficient background in the subject matter being discussed to convey this information correctly. As Danica Seleskovitch has observed, language-service professionals do not have to be experts in the subject matter of assignments they accept, but they must have the ability to make intelligent translation decisions on the basis of subject knowledge, both by preparing the topic and by grasping new information presented during the assignment. Therefore, we should examine whether majoring in a language is a necessary qualification for admission to advanced translation studies. Furthermore we may ask whether majoring in a language is a sufficient qualification for pursuing advanced translation studies. Employers requiring translation services often recruit students from foreign language departments, expecting them to perform capably as translators.

Variety of Disciplines

Participants in the study represented 29 majors. Because of this diversity, a more general grouping according to disciplines was used: languages, political science (including history), business, science, and the humanities. Figure 1 shows a comparison of students' performance according to this grouping by disciplines. The results are percentages of the subset of the sample having the same discipline.

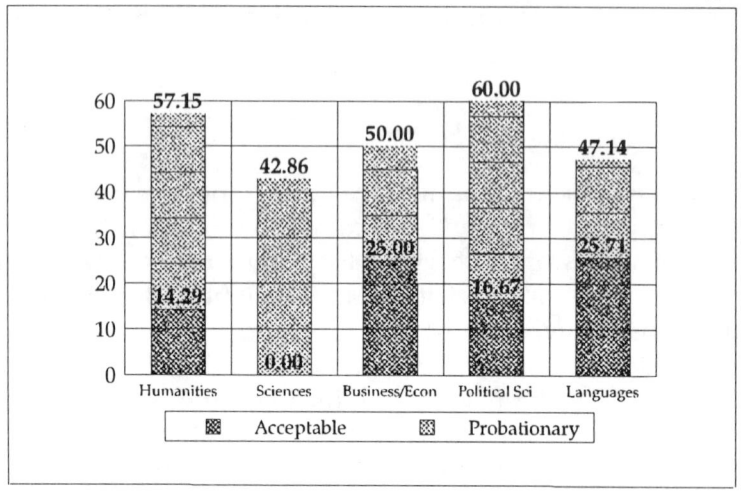

Figure 1. Successful Results, by Discipline

The percentage of participants rated acceptable in the business/economics category (e.g., those majoring in international business, international finance, and economics) was comparable to the distribution for those whose major was in a language. Both groups, the language and business students, had a greater proportion of "acceptable" results compared to participants from other disciplines. However, those with the greatest distribution of successful results in the study were the participants whose majors fell in the category of political science (e.g., history, international relations, area studies), although these participants had more borderline results than language or business majors. Humanities majors ran a close second in overall successful results, but also showed a lower percentage of acceptable scores. The higher percentage of borderline results in these two groups, however, indicates that these examinees may have mostly inferred from their subject knowledge, and their scanty language knowledge would occasionally deceive them. Those majoring in a science, on the whole, performed less well than the other groups in this study. It should be pointed out, however, that the number of business and science majors in this study was small; therefore the results in this respect may not be representative.

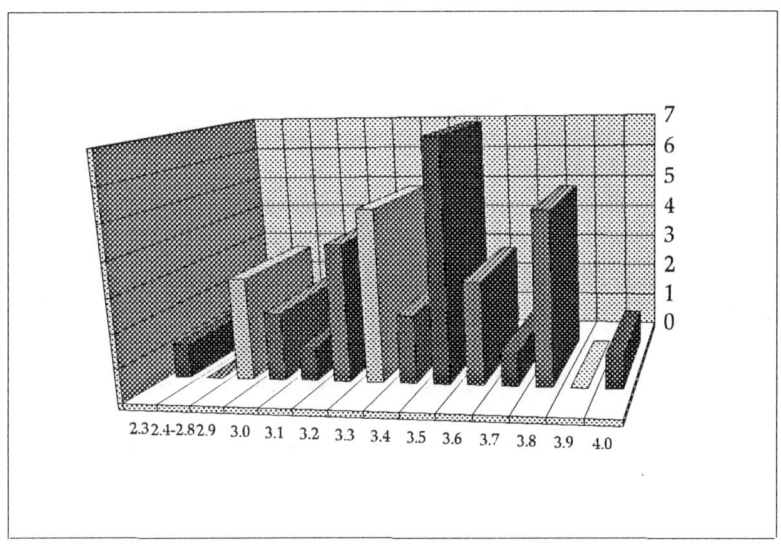

Figure 2.
Distribution of Unacceptable Language Majors, by G.P.A.

We also determined the frequency distribution of grade-point averages for those language majors rated unacceptable in the sample, as shown in figure 2. This chart excludes four candidates majoring in linguistics as the major does not necessarily involve in-depth study of a particular language. In the overall sample, there were unacceptable language majors with high grade-point averages. The chart shows that such instances cannot be discounted as aberrations. Therefore, it is clear that majoring in a language is not a sufficient criterion of readiness for advanced translation studies, even though the student may have a high grade-point average in the major.

The results by discipline indicate that majoring in a language is not necessarily a criterion for readiness to begin advanced translation studies. In fact, drawing on their area of studies seems to have enabled some non-language majors to score at least probationary results on the examination where others, majoring in a language but lacking this background were unsuccessful. More diversified coursework, then, may increase the number of candidates who are prepared to begin advanced translation studies. However, if the goal is to increase the number of students in the acceptable range—as indeed it seems it ought to be—students should not be advised to

80 Global Awareness and Language Learning

broaden their background knowledge at the expense of developing language mastery. Rather, it seems that a balanced mixture of the two is called for—a curriculum that builds both global awareness (through liberal arts and international studies) and strong language skills.

These considerations, however, have been drawn from observations about subsets of a sample, and are therefore quantitative. They provide guidelines for advising candidates as a group, in order to improve the distribution of overall results. However, the qualitative effect of background knowledge versus language skills for an individual over a given period of time has not been considered, and would be a worthwhile study in its own right.

The results, by language and class, are shown in both figure 3 and table 1.

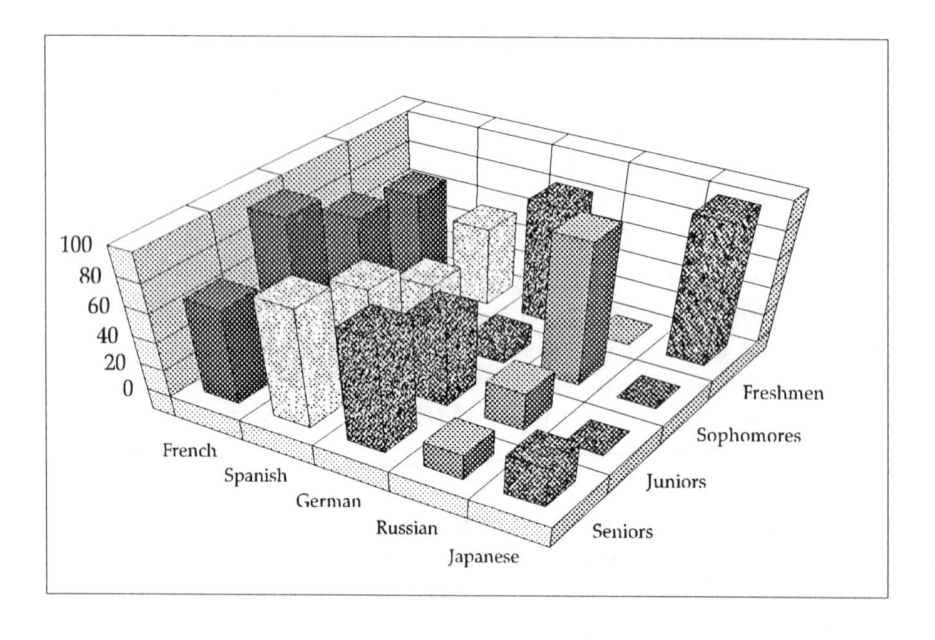

Figure 3. Successful Results, by Language and Class

Table 1. Translation Test Results, by Language and Class

	Unacceptable	Probationary	Acceptable
English into Japanese			
freshmen	100%	0%	0%
sophomores	0%	0%	0%
juniors	100%	0%	0%
seniors	100%	0%	0%
French into English			
freshmen	33.3%	50%	16.7%
sophomores	25%	75%	0%
juniors	0%	0%	100%
seniors	33.3%	0%	66.7%
German into English			
freshmen	16.7%	33.3%	50%
sophomores	85.7%	14.3%	0%
juniors	40%	40%	20%
seniors	16.7%	16.7%	66.7%
Japanese into English			
freshmen	0%	0%	100%
sophomores	0%	0%	0%
juniors	100.0%	0%	0%
seniors	71.4%	28.6%	0%
Russian into English			
freshmen	0%	0%	0%
sophomores	0%	33.3%	66.7%
juniors	72.7%	18.2%	9.1%
seniors	81.8%	18.2%	0%
Spanish into English			
freshmen	44.4%	33.3%	22.2%
sophomores	58.8%	29.4%	11.8%
juniors	33.3%	50%	16.7%
seniors	16.7%	50%	33.3%

Since all language students must take a placement test to be assigned appropriately to intensive, intermediate, or advanced language courses, the class is less significant for Georgetown's heterogeneous population than it would be for students who all come in at the same level in their first year. In some groups, a progression is recorded from first to fourth year.

Study Abroad

Study abroad is an important feature of education at Georgetown University. Also, its student population includes many children of diplomats who had part of their schooling abroad. Figure 4 shows the distribution of successful results as a percentage of the test population taking the examination and having studied abroad at or below the specified intervals of time. As the amount of time spent abroad decreases, the distribution of results among languages within Group I[1] exhibits less disparity, with the exception of German, which strongly falls below Spanish and French. Can there be too much of a good thing? In some cases, yes. Language interference between English and the Romance languages is a well documented phenomenon (see Cortese de Bosis, Kirk-Breene, Koessler and Derocquigny, Malone, Mascheroe and Zamarin, Thody and Evans). None of the students who were tested for Japanese into English had spent less

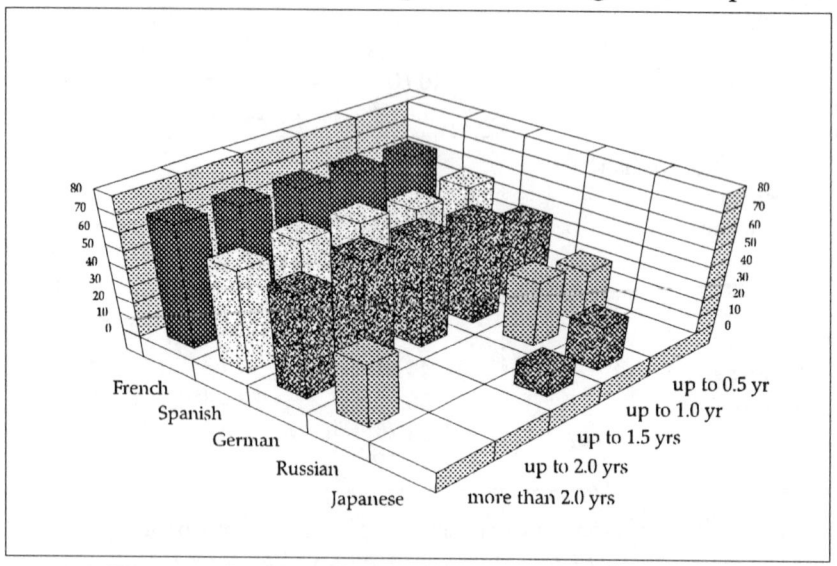

Figure 4. Test Results, by Periods of Study Abroad

than half a year abroad, so findings could not be recorded for this interval.

Study abroad programs are usually taken in the junior year, for either one semester or two. Therefore, what appears to be the influence of time spent abroad could, in fact, be attributable to differences in performance between class when compared within language combination. As table 1 indicates, no correlation between class and performance on the examination is discernible when considered according to individual language combinations.

These findings seem to show that study abroad exerts an influence on students' preparedness for translation studies. In the majority of the intervals considered, there was a correlation between time spent abroad and results on the examination. However, the exceptions to this correlation also show that time abroad is not a sufficient condition for readiness to begin translation studies. In fact, among those who were unsuccessful in the study were participants who had spent as much as fifteen years in a foreign country. Therefore, it is reasonable to consider study abroad as a contributory factor in the preparation of students for translation but not a sufficient preparation.

The distribution of results shown in figure 4 also reflects the interrelation of language combination and the effect of time spent abroad for the sample. The group of students working from German and having spent a half a year or less abroad showed a significantly lower distribution of successful results than their counterparts working from French or Spanish. For native speakers of English, working from German seems to pose special problems not found in Spanish or French. Boschen and Strasser have each shown in their research on Esperanto that a language that has a case system, forms numerous different plurals, is given to complex word compounds—some of which are misleading (e.g., *Wasserstoff* or *Eiweiß*), uses separable prefixes which can radically alter the meaning of a root, etc., is generally more difficult to learn. Evaluators for the German into English combination observed that failure to understand the effect of separable prefixes on the meaning of roots was responsible in several instances for a distorted translation.

Cultural and Geographic Differences

Most employers of translators and interpreters expect these professionals to have a broad cultural background. Along with the growth of intergovernmental organizations alone—the United Nations, the European Community, the Organization of American States, the Organization of African Unity, to name just a few—African and Caribbean studies have become part of this background. The modern international organizations which first employed conference interpreters and set up professional translation services were organizations of European countries, e.g., the League of Nations, the International Labor Office, and the United Nations. Between 1920 and 1945, interpretation was used mainly for delegates who shared a common Greco-Roman Judeo-Christian heritage, and the newly independent countries, after World War II, were keenly aware of these traditions, as shown by the official records of the UN General Assembly. Most of their representatives had gone through the schools and universities of the former colonial masters. But this influence in the educational systems of the Third World countries has been steadily declining. Regional organizations, e.g., the Organization of African Unity, have been creating a tradition of their own. Language professionals must be aware of both traditions, if they are to do justice to cultural innuendo and implicit information, metaphors and proverbs in the texts they translate.

From this viewpoint, students with a non-European background may benefit from their familiarity with more than one cultural tradition. Since there has been great concern that students belonging to non-European ethnic groups are being disenfranchised by an unaccommodating and Eurocentric academic system, for translation students from Africa and East Asia, Georgetown University has recognized their need to take courses in European history and culture. To the extent that American and European students have covered this material in secondary education, they have an advantage in college over their peers who must devote extra time to this area. Only in recent years has there been a trend to offer courses on hitherto-neglected aspects of world culture, e.g., "Middle Eastern and Asian Literary Traditions," taught by a team of specialists in Ancient Middle Eastern, Arabic, Chinese, Indian, Japanese, and Persian literature. It is thus a matter of interest whether there was a disparity in performance on the examination with regard to ethnic group. Participants were asked to specify the ethnic group to which they belong, although the study coordinators did not insist on a response if the participants were not comfortable answering this question.[2] 70.5% of the participants responded, and the findings take into account only this portion of the sample. We found that the Afro-American participants in this study performed slightly better than the white group in terms of acceptable results, and equally well in terms of probationary results. The results for the Asian and Hispanic groups were below the results for the other groups, but other factors may have adumbrated these findings. For the Hispanic group, 30% used only the source language at home. 20% of the Hispanics using the target language at home (10% of whom used Spanish as well) took the examination for source languages other than Spanish. Therefore, any benefit they might have had from exposure to Hispanic culture in their family settings would not have been of use to them for the test. Similar considerations applied to the Asian group. 14.3% of those who identified themselves as Asian in background used only the source language at home. 28.6% tested in a traditional European language, and thus for this group, too, any ethnic advantage they may have would not have been demonstrated on the examination. Moreover, the remainder of the Asian group was working with a combination involving Japanese, and most of them spoke English at home. Therefore, the difficulty factor for a native speaker of English to learn Japanese to the point where he can use it successfully for translation no doubt had a bearing on the results for the Asian group. In light of these considerations, the results for the Asian and Hispanic groups may have had less to do with ethnic background than with the language spoken at home and the language combination in which they tested.

More controlled testing is needed to ascertain whether exposure in the family setting to an Asian or Hispanic culture provides an advantage or disadvantage for students working with language combinations involving those cultures. Such a study would require eliminating the possibility that any disadvantage is due to the language used at home. Ideally, then, the population would have to at least speak the target language at home. And given that such students are minorities at American institutions, it will be difficult to attain a sufficient sampling that meets the conditions for such a study. However, the present findings suggest that such students may, indeed, be at a disadvantage when they speak only the source language in the family setting.

The results for the Afro-American participants in the study were highly encouraging. Concerns have been raised about evaluating Afro-Americans by a canon of "standard" English imposed by a predominantly white community. However, variations in English as used by the Afro-American community did not impair the ability of Afro-Americans in this study to perform favorably in comparison with other candidates.

Comparing Undergraduates to the Wider Population

So far, these comparisons have only considered performance by academic class. A comparison between the performance of the undergraduate population versus a more diversified sample may help put the undergraduate population's results in perspective. We used the results obtained by applicants to the division's programs over the three years of the study as the basis for our comparison. This population includes undergraduates, post-baccalaureates, and those who have never completed a first university degree but have professional experience to compensate for their lack of degree. The texts used at the examination were at a similar level of difficulty as those used for this study. The results for this group reflect the success rate by language combinations tested, not by individuals tested. Candidates at the division's entrance examinations may take the examination for more than one language combination if they choose. Each language combination is evaluated independently of any others the candidate may take during the examination session.

Table 2 shows the overall distribution of results for the two populations.

Table 2. Comparison of Translation-Program Applicants
to Undergraduate Population

	Acceptable	Probationary	Unacceptable
Undergraduate Population	27.17%	32.61%	40.22%
Program Applicants	40.91%	29.61%	29.48%

The analysis showed a marked disparity in performance between the undergraduate population and the usual applicant pool tested by the division. One very plausible account to explain these results is that, in many instances, the intellectual maturity required for advanced translation studies may be acquired only after undergraduate studies have been completed. Although no correlation between academic class and performance on the examination was ascertained in the stratified study, intellectual maturity should not be neglected in a group that includes higher age brackets. However, there is one very significant difference between the test population and the applicant pool from which the basis for comparison was derived: the latter group had chosen translation studies as its area of studies, whereas the majority of the test project sample did not intend to pursue translation studies. Furthermore, in the division's experience, undergraduates sometimes choose their major by a process of elimination. When their high school record is mediocre, but verbal skills are rated a few points higher, they opt for a language major. The difference in motivation between the two groups may have affected the distribution of results.

Conclusion

The findings quoted here have been based on the performance of Georgetown undergraduates. Similar studies in other academic settings would greatly extend the scope of these findings. In addition, longitudinal studies of student development would be a useful complement to the study undertaken here.

As a preliminary conclusion we can state that the single fact of majoring in a language in college is neither a necessary nor a sufficient criterion for qualifying for advanced translation studies. A broad liberal arts background, together with language knowledge, appears to be the most promising basis. Robert Lado wrote that "Learning a second language involves acquiring varying degrees of facility.... These facilities must be learned so that they can operate when attention is on the content and the thread of the argument and not on the expression items" (p. 39).

The overall approach we would like to see with regard to all stages of translation studies is demonstrable through an observation a number of years ago in a Club of Rome meeting on innovative learning: It is not sufficient to teach people to stop when the traffic light is red and to go when the light is green; you also want them to know what to do when the light is out of order.

Notes

[1] The group of languages which, according to the Foreign Service Institute of the U.S. Department of State, are easiest to learn for native speakers of English: among them the Romance languages and German. *Expected Levels of Absolute Speaking Proficiency in Languages Taught at the Foreign Service Institute*, revised April 1973.

[2] At the time the questionnaire was drawn up, "black" was the designation used by the Department of Health, Education, and Welfare for "Afro-American." Most of those in the Hispanic and Asian groups in this study were Hispanic-Americans from Latin American countries and Asian-Americans.

References

Boschen, A.C. "Esperanto, To Simplify and Clarify International Communication." *Communicating to the World*. Garden City, NY: Institute of Electrical and Electronics Engineers, 1989. 71–76.

Botkin, James W., Mahdi Elmandjra, and Mircea Malitza. *No Limits to Learning. Bridging the Human Gap. A Report to the Club of Rome*. Oxford: Pergamon Press, 1979.

Bowen, David. "The Intercultural Component in Interpreter and Translator Training; A Historical Survey." Diss. Georgetown University, 1985.

Bowen, Margareta. "Language Learning and Becoming a Professional Translator." *The Jerome Quarterly* 4.4 (1989): 2, 10–12.

———, and Patrick S. P. Lafferty. "Gender as a Factor in Undergraduate Translation Preparedness." *The Jerome Quarterly* 6.4 (1991): 7–11.

Cortese de Bosis, Alessandro. *Ostacoli della lingua inglese moderna / Obstacles of the Italian Language*. Rome: A. Signorelli, 1973(?).
Danchev, Andrei. "The Controversy over Translation in Language Teaching." Roundtable Discussion on Translation in Foreign Language Teaching. Paris: Fédération Internationale des Traducteurs–UNESCO, 1983.
Gomes de Matos, Francisco. "Human Rights Applied to Translation: A Case for Language Learners' Right to Translate." *Translation: Theory and Practice—Tension and Interdependence*. Ed. Mildred L. Larson. American Translators Association Scholarly Monograph Series 5. Binghamton, NY: SUNY-Binghamton P, 1991. 254–59.
Kirk-Breene, C[hristopher] W.E. *French False Friends*. London: Routledge and Kegan Paul, 1981.
Koessler, Maxime, and Jules Derocquigny. *Les faux amis: ou, les pièges du vocabulaire anglais*. Paris: Vuitbert, 1949.
Lado, Robert. *Language Teaching, a Scientific Approach*. New York: McGraw-Hill, 1964.
Malone, Joseph L. "False Friendship in International Language Planning." *Language Planning at the International Level*. Ed. Humphrey Tonkin and Karen Johnson-Weiner. New York: Center for Research and Documentation on World Language Problems, 1984. 17–26.
Mascheroe, Mario, and Laura Zamarin. *Op falses cognatos na traducão do ingles para o portugues*. 3d ed. São Paulo: Difei, 1980.
Newman, Patricia. "The Second Step." *The Jerome Quarterly* 4.2 (1989): 2, 13.
Seleskovitch, Danica. *Interpreting for International Conferences*. Trans. Stephanie Dailey and E. Norman McMillan. Washington, DC: Pen and Booth, 1978.
Strasser, Gerhard F. *Lingua universalis: Kryptologie und Theorie der Universalsprachen im 16. und 17. Jahrhundert*. Wiesbaden: O. Harrassowitz, 1988. 259–61. Wolfenbütteler Forschungen 39.
Thody, Philip, and Howard Evans, with Gwilym Rees. *Mistakable French: A Dictionary of Words and Phrases Easily Confused*. New York: Scribner, 1985.
Visson, Lynn. "Interpreter Training: The Stepchild of Language Teaching." This volume.
Weller, Georgeanne. "Some Polemic Aspects of Translation in Foreign Language Pedagogy Revisited." *Translator Training and Foreign Language Pedagogy*. Ed. Peter Krawutschke. American Translators Association Scholarly Monograph Series 3. Binghamton, NY: SUNY-Binghamton P, 1989. 39–50.

Interpreter Training:
The Stepchild of Language Teaching

Lynn Visson

I have three years of college Russian and I want to be an interpreter. Oh, by the way, I also know German. Maybe I could work at the UN.

Almost every month I get such calls from starry-eyed and enthusiastic college students recommended to me by former colleagues from the years I taught Russian language and literature at Columbia University and Bryn Mawr College. Though these students are sincere in saying that they want to be interpreters, through no fault of their own, their notion of what is involved here is about as realistic as their notion of how to go to Mars for the weekend. Language teachers on both the high school and college levels are all too aware of the drastic crunch in their profession and of the problem of jobs and careers for their students. They regularly mumble to their young charges that of course for those who are really dedicated there are careers in teaching (which in translation means willing to starve if necessary) and that for those who would like some *beurre* in the *haricots* there are great futures in "government" or "international organizations." In most cases, neither the instructor nor the student has any idea of what this means. In the case of Russian, with which I am most familiar, this glorious career all too often means sitting tucked away in a damp basement of the Department of Commerce or in a cubicle of the Library of Congress deciphering columns of fine print in crumbling issues of Russian provincial newspapers on corn production in Siberia over the last five years while dreaming of the era of *From Russia with Love*, cloaks and daggers, beautiful Russian blondes, glittering embassy parties, and a meteoric rise from reader of rotting newspapers to the rank of ambassador plenipotentiary.

It very rarely occurs to most teachers of Russian or of other foreign languages to suggest interpretation or translation as a more rewarding, creative, and lucrative career than the above-mentioned options, and when they do so, it is often with little knowledge of what is required or of the domestic job situation in this field. Interpreter training can be called the stepchild of language teaching since those educational institutions which could be the ideal place for rearing this child to professional adulthood instead prefer to concentrate on force-feeding their beloved biological children: reading, writing, speaking, and oral comprehension.

When a student says that he "knows" a language, he is usually referring to active knowledge, for he has been trained to believe that "knowing" a foreign language means speaking it, perhaps reading it, or acquiring the ability to order from a menu or write a simple letter. Very rarely does the student think of "knowing" a language in terms of the kind of passive, but nearly *total*, comprehension which is the most critical aspect of "knowing" the source language for the interpreter or translator. This knowledge consists not simply of the lexicon but also of the linguistic structure and what can broadly be called the "culture" of the country in which the language is spoken. The assumption that the interpreter must speak the source language as well as the target language with near-native fluency has scared off many a young would-be translator or interpreter. Nor does the foreign language teacher usually stress the crucial importance for the student of foreign languages and future translator-interpreter of mastery of one's own native tongue.

The other side of the coin is the happily bilingual student, who is told by all and sundry including his teachers that he will make a wonderful interpreter. In fact, because of their frequent inability to code switch, bilinguals often make extremely poor interpreters. They are fine in either of their two languages, but cannot make the shift across. (Of course, there are exceptions; some people from a very young age have been accustomed to switching languages and can in fact work into either language.) To use the language of the fairy tale, when they are good, they are very very good and when they are bad, they are horrid.

And yet language classes—both high school and college—could be the ideal training ground and petri dish for translators and interpreters. It is a rare first-year language course that does not make heavy use of some form of translation exercise. Unfortunately, even at advanced levels, these exercises tend to stress literal renderings of source into target language with little or no attention paid to the lexicon, syntax, and style of the target language, in this case English.

And it is no secret to anyone who has read student essays or listened to conversations propped up by halting interjections and phrases such as "so like then," "and then he goes," "uh, you know, like, you know what I mean," that very many American students have a rather feeble grasp of the grammar and style of their native language. Some courses stress the idea "don't translate: think in French, Russian, or whatever." While the intent of thinking in the language is noble, the function of translation exercises can be very positive, for the student stands to gain a great deal from intelligent translation exercises that make him more aware of the problems of grammar, vocabulary, syntax, and intonation—both in his own language and in the language he is studying.

Translation and interpretation are not popular options for American graduate students because of the dearth of professional schools and a lack of knowledge about them. In the US very few colleges and universities offer even elementary translation courses, and full programs are offered only by a handful of schools, such as Georgetown University or the Monterey Institute of International Studies, with a full program in Russian translation and interpretation offered only at Monterey. "Russian Translation" as a course title conveys very little information. Is this translation from Dostoyevsky or from *Известия* [*Izvestiia*]? It is most unlikely that language programs which have students reading Chekhov stories (often watered down), little anecdotes of John's summer trip to the USSR, and bits of *Правда* [*Pravda*] articles will produce qualified interpreters and translators. University language labs are also badly underused, though their equipment would be ideal for listening to tapes, working on comprehension, and practicing interpretation, even if on a fairly elementary level.

Nor is the situation helped by a rather outdated image of the interpreter in the US. While the mass media, and in particular television, have helped make the public more aware of interpreters—who has not seen the block print: "Voice of translator" appearing as subtitles on the news broadcasts—the image of the interpreter is still, as one observer put it, that of a "rather low-status individual. The image is of a middle-aged person in a shabby jacket who speaks English with a noticeable accent, and who is probably an immigrant to the United States" (Brislin, p. 27).

Yet another problem is the lack of practical literature in English on interpretation. While there are plenty of theoretical works, studies of neurology, semiotics, *langue et parole*, etc., there is a real lack of practical manuals, texts, and exercise books with which the aspiring student could practice translation or interpretation. When I set about writing *From Russian into English: An Introduction to Simultaneous Interpretation*, I realized that I was writing in a nearly total vacuum. There is a great need for practical translation-interpretation manuals for French, German, Spanish, and other modern languages with which students could practice and develop a taste for these professions as well as advance their language skills.

Working with translation, e.g., from Russian, gives students a greater distance from both Russian and English. They become aware of the problem of tenses, since the truncated Russian tense system requires that the English speaker constantly choose between compound and continuous tenses. Students must recognize that Russian syntax introduces new information after old information and that the intonation patterns of the two languages are totally different. Such exercises expand the students' linguistic horizons and make them more sensitive to vocabulary, syntax, and style, even if they never become professional translators or interpreters.

The student can be trained to get away from words, which are both the best friends and worst enemies of the interpreter, and made to start thinking in terms of meaning and context. What does the word "shot," for example, mean in English? How should it be translated? A shot can be a gun going off, a glass of vodka, an injection, a photograph, an impetus, or a space launch. Let alone idioms, such as a shot in the dark, I'm shot, shot through, take a shot at, or to shoot oneself in the foot. Once the student stops thinking in terms of "how do you translate this word or phrase" and starts thinking of "what does this mean?" or "what is the specific linguistic, cultural, political, and social context here?" he is on his way to a greater linguistic and literary sensitivity, and a greater understanding of the nuances of language and culture. To take one of the thousands of examples of the problem of cultural rather than linguistic equivalents, what about the Russian and English connotations of the words "communal apartment"? As the translator Richard Lourie has commented,

> The translator's heart sinks at the sight of words like *kommunalka*, which he knows he must render as "communal apartment." ... The English term conjures up an image of a Berkeley, California, kitchen where hippies with headbands are cooking brown rice, whereas the Russian term evokes a series of vast brown rooms with a family living in each, sharing a small kitchen where the atmosphere is dense with everything that cannot be said and the memory of everything that shouldn't have been said, but was. (Lourie and Mikhailov, p. 38)

Or take the useful Russian concept of реалия [realiia], all those phenomena which exist in one culture without direct equivalents in another. These provide excellent examples for "cultural" translation, such as the Russian дом отдыха [dom otdyxa], which if literally translated as "rest home" suggests a geriatrically inclined convalescent institution, when in fact it is the equivalent of a holiday center or resort.

The student who wants to be an interpreter needs not just nouns and verbs but also cultural connectives, knowledge of the history, geography, economics, and literature of the country whose language he is studying. He needs a broad cultural background, for the interpreter may find himself facing quotes from the *Wall Street Journal*, Walt Whitman, the Bible and the Koran, *Pravda*, and Cervantes.

Campuses are natural crossroads and waystations for exchange programs and visitors, and giving students a chance to practice escort interpreting with foreign visitors can be an enormously exciting experience. Organizations such as the "Experiment in International Living" and numerous NGOs have played a crucial role here. Interpretation provides the student with the instant and immediate gratification that translation cannot supply, the thrill of actually facilitating two-way communication and seeing the results. At professional congresses, such as AATF for French teachers, or AATSEEL for Russian teachers, instructors should be made aware of the existence of the State Department Language Services division, the USIA, the UN language services departments, and of private interpretation-translation agencies. This will enable them to give students a more realistic view of these professions and help guide capable candidates into these fields and keep the unqualified ones out.

Awareness of the existence of real jobs and careers can stimulate the creation of translation and interpretation courses, summer seminars, and graduate programs. Most language teachers are unaware that UN interpreters into English must work from either Russian and French or French and Spanish, and that they must know both languages equally well. Most free-lance interpreters also try to work with at least three languages. Awareness of these requirements can stimulate students to study a second language and universities to provide additional instruction facilities.

UN materials could be invaluable aids to language teachers, whether or not they are in the business of urging their students to become translators and interpreters. UN documents published in the organization's six official languages, if provided with glosses, notes, and exercises, could be the basis for compiling anthologies and could introduce students to the political, economic, and social realities of our day as well as add to their knowledge of languages. Tapes of speeches—either original UN tapes or excerpts from speeches read by native speakers in the original language—can similarly support language teaching. The UN television films in the various languages, which are often shown in UN language classes, could be extremely useful to high school and college language students. With all its documents, literature, and films translated into the six official languages, the UN is an untapped storehouse of foreign-language teaching materials which could be used by university language-teaching operations to interest students in eventually working for international organizations. Making language teachers more aware of the professions of translator and interpreter would enrich language classes, and a university campus with well-informed instructors could provide fertile soil and an excellent training ground for future professionals. Perhaps then this Cinderella stepchild will acquire the legitimacy of a full-fledged member of the linguistic family.

References

Brislin, Richard W., ed. *Translation: Applications and Research.* New York: Gardner, 1976.

Lourie, Richard, and Aleksei Mikhailov. "Why You'll Never Have Fun in Russian." *The New York Times Book Review,* 18 June 1989, p. 38.

Visson, Lynn. *From Russian into English: An Introduction to Simultaneous Interpretation.* Ann Arbor, Michigan: Ardis, 1991.

Linguistic Pluralism for Internationalization: The Case for Non-Traditional Approaches to Language Study for U.S. Schools

Timothy Reagan and Karen Case

There can be little doubt that for the vast majority of students in the United States foreign language education has been a failure. Individuals educated in the United States tend to have brief and ineffective exposure to languages other than English in the public schools, and they overwhelmingly remain monolingual. The old joke that a person who speaks three languages is a trilingual, one who speaks two languages is a bilingual, and one who speaks only one language is an American, is far too close to reality to be very funny. Furthermore, not only do students in the United States not learn other languages, but what they generally do appear to learn is that competence in a second language is both unnecessary and unusual—perhaps even "strange." Both of us have actually heard university faculty argue against even minimal foreign language requirements for undergraduates on the grounds that such study is "a waste of students' time and money." Indeed, competence in a second language is to some degree viewed with suspicion. Recent efforts to make English the official language of the United States, for instance, often make use of advertisements that imply that bilingualism or linguistic pluralism may pose a threat to national unity, and that individuals who would prefer to function in a language other than English are in some sense un-American (see Crawford). Finally, for the small percentage of students in the United States who actually do study a foreign language in school, the options from which they can choose seldom go beyond the standard Western European languages, and they are rarely able seriously to pursue foreign language study before the completion of their elementary school experience.

The results of this failure of foreign language education in the United States have been widely discussed. It is clear, at least to those who will listen, that the United States is placed at a serious disadvantage in economic terms in the international and global marketplace, that national security is often compromised by our lack of foreign language skills, and, perhaps most important, that our ignorance of other languages and cultures, coupled with what can be termed our national arrogance, is rapidly cutting us off from the global community in a host of cultural, educational, and social ways. Senator Paul Simon's excellent book, *The Tongue-Tied American: Confronting the Foreign Language Crisis*, has made these points far better and more powerfully than we can, and his documentation of fiasco after fiasco related to American ignorance of foreign languages ought to concern us all. Whether the problem is selling cars called "it won't go" (Nova) in Latin America, offering to bring your ancestors back from the grave (Pepsi) in the PRC, or simply not having any speakers of Russian on hand at the US embassy in Kabul as Soviet troops crossed the border, this lack of linguistic competence is clearly a growing problem for American society.

The focus of our presentation is not, however, to build a case for foreign language education, nor is it to assess blame for the current state of affairs. Rather, we want to begin with a somewhat different (and perhaps even heretical) premise from that generally assumed by foreign language advocates, and then to offer some suggestions for some admittedly incremental changes that may help, in the long run, to improve the foreign language learning situation in the United States. At the outset, though, we want to emphasize that as former foreign language teachers, we are both deeply committed to traditional foreign language courses and programs, and believe that it is essential that they continue for those students we can attract to them. Our suggestions are not intended to serve as replacements for traditional foreign language instruction, but rather, as a way of making such instruction more attractive and worthwhile.

The basic, and heretical, premise that we would like to offer is that given the nature of contemporary US society, attitudes about and toward foreign languages and foreign language education are unlikely to change in the near or intermediate term, regardless of how compelling and practical the arguments in favor of such change might be. Most Americans will continue to see foreign language education as, at best, a nice "frill" in a child's schooling, and few parents will actively support early and extensive instruction in a language other than English. Further, relatively few students will be willing or able to devote the years necessary to develop meaningful competence in a second language, and most foreign language students will cease their study of a foreign language before such competence is achieved.

What we wish to suggest, then, is an alternative that can be directed toward all children in the schools in order to change attitudes about languages other than English, as well as to provide some knowledge about languages and language diversity in general terms and to promote an interest in language learning among a greater proportion of students than is now the case. Such objectives are actually fairly low-level; we are basically suggesting that we try to teach *about* other languages initially, rather than attempting to introduce basic foreign language training for all students at some point (an alternative that understandably has a considerable amount of support among foreign language educators in the United States). As a starting point, what we are assuming is that, as Gardner and Clement have recently suggested, "different training programmes may be more suited to some patterns of abilities than to others ... [and] that language educators should consider matching particular programmes to particular ages and ability groupings" (p. 498) and, further, that such differences in aptitude and readiness for foreign language study can perhaps be best assessed and addressed in nontraditional ways. Toward this end, we want briefly to outline five different approaches that might achieve the sort of educational objective we are advocating, as well as raising some of the problems and limitations of each.

The "Linguistics for Kids" Approach

One potentially useful way of exposing children to foreign languages in a relatively non-threatening manner while supporting the existing language arts curriculum, is to introduce the study of language and languages into the curriculum. In essence, we suggest that children be taught some of the basic ideas and themes of modern linguistics. Needless to say, we are not suggesting that third graders should learn the ins and outs of transformational grammar, nor is there any reason for high school students to learn the intricacies of raising or of pronominalization. However, students at both the elementary and secondary levels would benefit from the study of the general nature of human languages, the development and evolution of languages, orthographies and the ways in which languages can be (and are) written, lexical expansion and borrowing, and so on, in both language arts and social studies classes. Charles Berlitz's book *Native Tongues* would be a valuable teacher resource in this regard. Also possible in such a "linguistics for kids" approach might be the brief study of a "language of the day," for which a teacher might use Kenneth Katzner's *The Languages of the World* as a guide and resource. The study of such a "language of the day" would allow for discussion of geography, history, religion, and literature, as well as such clearly linguistic themes as language family, orthography, and so on. Finally, in a language arts or English class, students might study language evolution by contrasting the development of English from Anglo-Saxon to Middle English to Modern English with that of other languages, with an emphasis on the influence of other languages on language change (see Clark, Jones).

This approach has many advantages and benefits, but it is certainly not without problems as well. Perhaps the most serious deficiency is that it does not actually involve language study; it would be possible for such a program to be implemented by teachers with no language skills themselves (although one might also consider this one of its strengths). Further, while if successful, such an approach would have the positive additional benefit of encouraging team-teaching across disciplinary lines, the lack of such team-teaching could easily mitigate any positive outcomes. Finally, it is possible that many teachers would perceive such an approach as involving irrelevant additional content in their own subject-matter areas. In short, for this approach to function effectively, changes would be required not only to student attitudes, but also most probably to those of their parents and teachers.

At the same time, an initial "linguistics for kids" approach in the elementary school might well provide a valuable foundation for further, specific language study. For instance, this approach might well be used to prepare students for entry into more traditional FLES or FLEX approaches (see Lipton).

The "Willkommen, Bienvenu, Bienvenida" Approach

A second approach to exposing students to language study, and one which already exists both formally and informally in some elementary schools, generally under the label "FLEX," is that of providing students with a brief introduction to several commonly taught foreign languages. Where such an approach is used, children most often learn songs in the target language as well as very basic vocabulary (greetings, colors, days of the week, and so on). Thus, students might study German for a few months, followed by a few months of French, followed by a few months of Spanish. If properly implemented, such an approach can make foreign language learning fun for children, and thus may predispose them to additional foreign language study later on. A further benefit may be that this approach would involve bringing other (presumably bilingual) adult role models into the classroom (assuming, as is generally the case, that the classroom teacher is not competent in a language other than English). To some extent, young children in elementary schools today are already primed for such exposure as a result of similar efforts on *Sesame Street* (where Spanish is used on occasion) and other children's television programs. Finally, since such exposure programs generally require little time, parents tend to be supportive of them. With older students, the "Willkommen" approach can be used to present the options for foreign language study in a particular school, and thus can serve a dual function both to encourage language study in general and to help students make somewhat more informed choices as they consider studying specific foreign languages. Finally, an approach of this type raises relatively few certification-related issues, since the regular classroom teacher in the elementary-school context normally suffices to meet the legal requirement for a certified professional—that is, where community members are used, the classroom teacher remains the certified professional in the room.

There are, however, several drawbacks to such programs. First of all, since they focus on language exposure, any effect that they do have on children's attitudes toward other languages are tangential to what actually takes place in the classroom. Further, they do not actually provide any meaningful or particularly useful base for further language study, and may end up inadvertently trivializing foreign languages and foreign language study. This is especially likely where the classroom teacher him/herself, whose second language skills may be weak at best, attempts to teach the target language or languages alone. At the present time, some 22% of all elementary school students in the United States study a foreign language at school, and most of these select students will achieve only a minimal proficiency in the language at best (see Tucker, 1990). This limitation can be attributed to a number of factors. The monolingual child is confronted with a variety of problems and barriers on his/her way to acquiring proficiency in a second language. Among the problems are a lack of adequately funded programs, the absence of articulation between elementary and secondary programs, and, in all too many cases, the expectation that the child should master grammatical forms rather than gain communicative competence in the target language. Often, too, foreign language instruction in the United States emphasizes the study of language as an end in itself (Tucker), rather than as a means for acquiring new knowledge and intergroup understanding and communication (Padilla, Fairchild, and Valadez). All too often, in fact, the result of successful foreign language programs is, as Humphrey Tonkin has so articulately put it, the production of individuals who are bilingually and biculturally chauvinistic. Finally, by emphasizing the foreign languages normally taught in the school district, such programs serve to reinforce the commonly held notion that these are the only other languages that are really worthy of respect and serious consideration.

The "Molo, Dumela, Sakubona" Approach[1]

This model addresses the last concern mentioned with respect to the "Willkommen" approach; the basic idea remains the same, with students being exposed briefly to a variety of different foreign languages. However, instead of studying the "standard" languages of Western Europe, an effort is made to find speakers of more "exotic" languages. Thus, children might be exposed to Chinese, Hindi, Hopi, Japanese, Russian, Zulu, or whatever language the teacher and the school can find a volunteer to teach. As with the "Willkommen" approach, of course, students will not actually gain any substantive proficiency in the target languages. They will, however, have been exposed to languages about which most Americans have at best very limited knowledge, and will have been taught that the variety of languages worthy of respect and study is far greater than the selection they are likely to have as public school students. Given the focus on "exotic" languages in this approach, it is also less likely that classroom teachers with marginal skills will try to present the language on their own, since they are unlikely to have studied such languages at all themselves. Certification issues here are the same as in the "Willkommen" approach.

Although this approach does deal effectively with some of the problems identified with the "Willkommen" approach, it nevertheless is faced with a number of other problems. It shares with the "Willkommen" approach limits with regard to the tangential relationship of changes in attitude to classroom activities, as well as most likely failing to provide a significant base for further language study. Most serious, though, is that, to even a greater extent than the "Willkommen" model, this approach may risk the trivialization of the target languages, especially if they are in fact seen by parents and/or teachers as really "irrelevant" to the child's needs and life experience. By the same token, if the languages are carefully selected, they may reinforce other aspects of the curriculum. For instance, if a school is seeking to develop and implement an Afrocentric curriculum (see Asante), the inclusion of brief units devoted to teaching children something about Ibo, Swahili, and Zulu, representing to some extent the diversity of languages in sub-Saharan Africa, for instance, might be valuable. Finally, it is possible that initial exposure to such "exotic" languages might lead, ultimately, to an expansion in language offerings at advanced levels.

The "Sign Language" Approach

Many teachers of young children are currently making efforts to teach basic fingerspelling and sign language in the school, and such attempts generally have parental support as well as reinforcement from various children's television shows (see Bove). Young children seem to enjoy such activities, and so there is clearly potential for positive teaching about languages, language diversity, and language learning. What is odd about the existing efforts is not that they are informal, nor that the teachers themselves are rarely proficient signers. Rather, what is strange is that teachers, students, and parents fail to see such instruction as related to *language*. One of the reasons for this is no doubt that most classroom teachers, like most hearing people in general, are woefully ill-informed about the nature and types of sign language (see, e.g., Reagan). "Signing" is somehow considered to be merely another modality in which English can be presented; thus, it takes on the form of a game that is useful in psychomotor development. Instruction in sign language is without question useful when understood in this way, but such an understanding not only distorts the nature of sign language and carries with it undesirable messages about the deaf in our society, it also misses an excellent opportunity for teaching children about language differences and language diversity. Properly utilized in a classroom setting with young children, sign language instruction can convey important messages about diversity, communication, and language that can serve as a basis for later language learning—whether sign language or a spoken foreign language. Valuable resources for younger children would be Linda Bove's *Sign Language Fun* and Bahan and Dannis' *Signs for Me*, as well as guides to teaching children to sign popular songs (see Galding et al.; Weaks); also useful (although only indirectly and implicitly concerned with issues of language and communication) is Shel Silverstein's poem "Deaf Donald," from his collection of poems, *A Light in the Attic* (p. 141). For older children, more formal approaches to sign language learning and teaching can be used, again both to teach about human language and communication and to provide a practical base for language learning. Useful in this regard would be Laura Greene and Eva Dicker's *Discovering Sign Language*. With high school age students, any of the great variety of sign language textbooks currently available could be easily and effectively used in the classroom.

The "Universalist" Approach

The last approach we will suggest here is somewhat different from the others we have discussed thus far. As a means of encouraging language study, as well as a way of introducing students at both the elementary and the secondary level to issues related to language diversity and human communication, it is possible to teach a selected language that can serve as a base for other language study. The idea here is essentially that all students could begin language study with a language that would be relatively easy to learn, and which would support later study of other foreign languages. Although traditionally in American education, Latin was the language most commonly associated with such arguments, its popularity, although of late making a comeback, remains limited. A viable alternative to Latin, and one which has the double advantage of ease of acquisition and an international/global orientation is, of course, Esperanto (see Tonkin). There are now materials available for teaching Esperanto that are reasonably useful for the classroom (Richardson's is an excellent text in this regard; also usable, though not without pedagogical limitations, are Butler and Cresswell and Hartley, and strong arguments for Esperanto's use in public schools have been offered.

Despite its advantages, however, numerous arguments can be presented against the use of Esperanto. First of all, there is the problem of reasonably trained (and appropriately certified) teachers. To put it kindly, it is unlikely that there would be competent users of Esperanto in most American public schools, and so the challenge of locating instructors presents a number of problems. Further, support for Esperanto is neither common nor particularly deep in most communities, though of course those involved in the Esperantist movement are very committed to the language and its propagation. Finally, it is possible in some US communities that objections may surface to Esperanto's internationalist nature—objections which probably lie just beneath the surface where other languages are concerned, but which can become focal points for resistance in the case of Esperanto. The view of languages other than English as suspect, and their speakers as somehow foreign and thus untrustworthy, has a tradition in American history—a tradition most clearly seen, perhaps, in the widespread rejection of the German language during the First World War which involved not only the elimination of German language classes in many public schools but even the burning of German books. Nonetheless, there is much to commend the study of an international language such as Esperanto, as well as the study of the history of efforts to create an international language (see Large;

also interesting here is Wood), and such options should certainly be considered.

Conclusion

Our concern has been to suggest some ways in which interest in languages, language study, and human communication broadly conceived might be encouraged in the American public schools. We believe that by encouraging such emphases in both elementary and secondary schools, a fundamental base can be provided upon which students can eventually build foreign language competence, if they choose—and which will at the very least support tolerance of language diversity and sensitivity to and awareness of language rights on the part of others where students choose not to study foreign languages themselves. In short, it would be our hope that we in the schools could do a better job of communicating the wisdom conveyed by a bumper-sticker we once saw. On a car no doubt owned by a foreign language teacher, the bumper-sticker declared, "Monolingualism is curable." Indeed it is, but as with all such treatments, one has to *want* the cure. We believe that it is time to begin helping students want the cure.

Note

[1]The terms used in the title for this section are, respectively, Xhosa (*Molo*), Northern Sotho (*Dumela*), and Zulu (*Sakubona*) terms for "good morning."

References

Asante, Molefi. *Afrocentricity: The Theory of Social Change*. Buffalo: Amulefi, 1980.
———. *The Afrocentric Idea*. Philadelphia: Temple UP, 1987.
———. *Kemet, Afrocentricity, and Knowledge*. Trenton: Africa World Press, 1990.
———. "The Afrocentric Idea in Education." *Journal of Negro Education* 60.2 (1991): 170–80.
Bahan, Ben, and Joe Dannis. *Signs for Me: Basic Sign Vocabulary for Children*. Berkeley: Dawn Sign Press, 1990.
Berlitz, Charles. *Native Tongues*. New York: Grosset and Dunlap, 1982.

Bove, Linda. *Sign Language Fun*. New York: Random House/Children's Television Workshop, 1980.
Butler, Montagu. *Step By Step in Esperanto*, 8th Ed. London: Esperanto Publishing, 1965.
Clark, John. *Early English: An Introduction to Old and Middle English*. New York: Norton, 1957.
Crawford, James. *Hold Your Tongue: Bilingualism and the Politics of "English Only."* Reading, MA: Addison-Wesley, 1992.
Cresswell, John, and John Hartley. *Teach Yourself Esperanto*. New York: McKay, 1968.
Galding, Donna, Daniel Pokorny, and Lottie Riekehof. *Lift Up Your Hands: Songs in Sign Language*. Washington, DC: The National Grange, 1976.
Gardner, Robert, and Clement, Richard. "Social Psychological Perspectives on Second Language Acquisition." *Handbook of Language and Social Psychology* Ed. H. Giles and W. Robinson. (London: Wiley, 1990). 495–517.
Greene, Laura, and Dicker, Eva. *Discovering Sign Language*. Washington, DC: Kendall Green Publications/Gallaudet UP, 1981.
Jones, Richard Foster. *The Triumph of the English Language*. Stanford: Stanford UP, 1953.
Katzner, Kenneth. *The Languages of the World*. New York: Funk and Wagnalls, 1975.
Large, Andrew. *The Artificial Language Movement*. Oxford: Basil Blackwell, 1985.
Lipton, Gladys C. *Practical Handbook to Elementary Foreign Language Programs*, 2nd Ed. Lincolnwood, IL: National Textbook, 1992.
Padilla, A., H. Fairchild, and C. Valadez, (Eds.). *Foreign Language Education: Issues and Strategies*. Newbury Park, CA: Sage, 1990.
Reagan, Timothy. "American Sign Language and Contemporary Deaf Studies in the United States." *Language Problems and Language Planning* 10.3 (1986): 282–89.
Richardson, David. *Esperanto: Learning and Using the International Language*. El Cerrito, CA: Esperanto League for North America, 1988.
Silverstein, Shel. *A Light in the Attic*. New York: Harper and Row, 1981.
Simon, Paul. *The Tongue-Tied American: Confronting the Foreign Language Crisis*. New York: Continuum, 1980.
Tonkin, Humphrey. *Introduction to Esperanto Studies*. Rotterdam: Esperanto Documents 6-A, 1976.
Tucker, G. R. "Second Language Education: Issues and Perspectives." In Padilla, Fairchild, and Valadez. 13–21.
Weaks, Donna. *Lift Up Your Hands: Popular Songs in Sign Language*, Vol. 2. Washington, DC: The National Grange, 1980.
Wood, Richard E. *Current Work in the Linguistics of Esperanto*. Rotterdam: Esperanto Documents 28-A, 1982.

Integrating Language Study and Global Education

Ronald J. Glossop

Why is it so difficult to integrate the study of foreign languages with global education? The basic difficulty is that global education is focused on informational content already available in the native language while using a foreign language constitutes a skill which usually requires several years of study to develop. In global education children are expected to learn about the beliefs, attitudes, and customs of people in various parts of the world and to acquire knowledge about differences in topography and climate and their impact on the society in various parts of the world. Such information can be acquired immediately in the pupil's native language, so why put off learning that material for several years while the child is developing the skill of using some other language?

Language study also raises some further questions, especially in schools in lands where the first language is English. Which foreign language should children be taught? Should it be Arabic, Chinese, French, German, Japanese, Russian, Spanish, or something else? How can we know which language or languages the child is going to need as an adult? And should they all be taught the same language?

Another problem occurs for smaller schools. It is the very practical problem of acquiring and maintaining the requisite critical mass of students who want to study the same language so that a class can be formed. If some of the children's parents want French, some want German, some Spanish, and so on, there may not be enough students desiring one particular language to warrant forming a single class for which a teacher could be hired. On the other hand, if the school decides to overcome this problem by using expensive individualized instruction relying on computers and videotapes, it still has the problem of finding teachers to answer the pupil's questions about all these various languages.

Still another problem is that even major languages are not really "global," so the foreign language student learns about some other parts of the world but not about the whole world. Arabic, Chinese, Japanese, and Russian will be helpful with regard to certain regions of the Earth's surface but not others. Even more widely used languages such as French and Spanish are not helpful in Asia and most of eastern Europe. English seems to be more "global" than any of the others.

And therein lies still another temptation to ignore foreign language study in schools where the first language is English. Why not just use English to establish penpal relationships with other children all over the world, even in non-English speaking countries? After all, there are children all over the world studying English. Their teachers and parents are very happy to have correspondence and videotape exchanges with other children who are native speakers of English. Since these other children are all over the world, it seems that the English-speaking children can get a global education from international correspondence with other children just using English. Why make things difficult by trying to get them to learn another language, which would be mastered only after several years of study?

Obviously, this way of proceeding is unacceptable. With such an arrangement our English-speaking children are not learning a foreign language while the children in the other countries are. But this approach to global education is even worse than just depriving our children of the experience of learning a foreign language that other children will have. In such a situation our English-speaking children are learning *from their own experience that they do not need to learn any other languages!* They are learning right in school that they can communicate with people all over the world using English. Under these circumstances both they and their parents will quickly conclude that foreign language study is a waste of time.

Fortunately, there is an alternative solution whereby foreign language study becomes intimately connected with global education. It is especially applicable to schools in English-speaking countries, but it is also useful in other lands because it takes those youngsters such a long time before they can use English well enough to participate in the international correspondence which is so basic to first-hand global education. This solution is to teach Esperanto to elementary school children all over the world.

Why will Esperanto work so much more effectively than other

languages? Because it can be learned so quickly compared to any other language. After only a few months of instruction, the children will be able to use Esperanto for exchanging cards and letters with children in many other countries. To be sure they will still depend on dictionaries, both when reading the letters they receive and when writing the letters they send, but they can do so with a minimal amount of assistance from the teacher. Only people who have some familiarity with Esperanto and experience in teaching the language to children can understand how that happens.

There are several reasons Esperanto can be learned and used quickly for actual correspondence. The most important is that there are absolutely no irregularities. Once a rule is learned, the students can rush ahead with no fear that they will encounter some exceptions about which they have not yet learned. They will make inferences about the language which will almost always turn out to be correct, an exciting situation for both pupil and teacher. From experience I can say that the major difficulties they have are due to the irregularities of their native language which drop out in Esperanto. For example, it takes a while for young native speakers of English to realize that "I *am*," "you *are*," and "he *is*," turn out in Esperanto to be "mi *estas*," "vi *estas*," and "li *estas*."

Another reason that Esperanto is so easily learned is that it is absolutely phonetic. There aren't even any combinations of letters to remember such as "c-h" or "e-a-u". In Esperanto each letter always has the same sound, even the vowels. Each syllable has one and only one vowel, and every multi-syllable word is accented on the next-to-last syllable. Thus the students learn the written language and the oral language together. They can figure out how to spell a word they have heard but never seen in written form. They can figure out how to correctly pronounce a word they have never seen or heard. Several years ago I had the experience of having a young man who had learned Esperanto completely from written lessons successfully converse with me, and this incident is by no means unique in the history of Esperanto.

Still another reason Esperanto can be learned so quickly is the elegant system of prefixes and suffixes which allows for systematic word-building for the writer and for rule-guided word-decoding for the reader. By using these prefixes and suffixes, a learner encountering one root acquires the basis for learning several words. Thus vocabulary grows by leaps and bounds. It is a great delight for the pupils to create and decipher words using these prefixes and suffixes with their carefully prescribed meanings. Learning vocabulary is fun rather than drudgery.

Esperanto also has the value of forcing pupils to learn grammar as they learn the language. As a result they become better prepared to study other languages later. Students of Esperanto learn grammar because the language is grammar-coded. All nouns end in "-o," all adjectives end in "-a," any word that ends in "-e" is an adverb, and so on. There is an accusative case for direct objects, so pupils must attend to this facet of sentence construction.

One of the tragedies with regard to language instruction is the mistaken belief that Esperanto is somehow the "enemy" of other languages. Nothing could be further from the truth. Having had a successful experience in language learning with Esperanto, having learned about language and grammar by virtue of their study of Esperanto, young people will be more willing and able to undertake the study of other languages, and they will learn them faster than the pupils who have not studied Esperanto.[1] I think high school teachers of foreign language should advocate Esperanto in the elementary schools as a base for beginning the study of national languages in middle or high school.

Because Esperanto can be used so quickly, children can start carrying on correspondence with children in other countries after a month or two. Global education does not need to be postponed for a year or two. As the pupils begin getting postcards from all over the world, language learning and learning about the rest of the world reinforce one another. The pupils want to better their skill in using Esperanto, and they want to learn more about that other country from which the postcard or letter came. The language becomes both the vehicle and the motivator for global eduation. An unanticipated consequence in one such program at the H. D. Cooke Elementary School in Washington, DC, was that the pupils wanted to learn more about their own community so that they could tell about it in the letters they were sending to children in other countries.

A welcome situation for the teacher who wants to embark on a program of teaching Esperanto as a vehicle for global education is that networks for locating penpals all over the world (including other teachers who are teaching Esperanto to their pupils) already exist. There are three functioning organizations whose focus is international child-to-child correspondence using Esperanto. One is the Kastora Klubo (Beaver Club) in Warsaw, Poland.[2] Another is "Infanoj Ĉirkaŭ la Mondo" (Children around the World) in San Diego, California.[3] The most recently developed is the network of teachers instructing Esperanto under the coordination of the "Esperanto" Radikala Asocio in Rome, Italy.[4] One can also acquire names and addresses from *Juna Amiko* (*Young Friend*), a quarterly magazine for children and young adults published in Hungary,[5] as well as *Kara Amiko* (*Dear Friend*), published by Poland's Kastora Klubo.

In the United States, another source of names and addresses of teachers and pupils of Esperanto around the world (and also other valuable information for teachers) is the quarterly *Bulteno* (*Bulletin*) of the American Association of Teachers of Esperanto.[6] American teachers working with 7th-grade gifted pupils might want to learn about the program for teaching Esperanto to such students used since 1982 by Gail Martin in the Seneca Ridge Middle School, Sterling, Virginia.[7] Teachers can obtain dictionaries and materials for adults from the Esperanto League for North America.[8]

Very good instructional materials are also available. In San Diego, Charlotte Kohrs has developed some excellent texts, including *Dek Demandoj* (*Ten Questions*), *La Bela Planedo* (*The Beautiful Planet*), and *Ni Parolu Esperanton Kune* (*Let Us Speak Esperanto Together*). Especially relevant to global education is Kohrs's booklet *Ni esploru la mondon* (*Let Us Explore the World*). This booklet contains two pages each about Britain, Czechoslovakia, China, Finland, France, Lithuania, Poland, and the U.S., consisting of questions and answers provided by the children of these countries. This booklet is a perfect example of how global education and language learning can be combined when one uses Esperanto.

Charlotte Kohrs has also written songs to help pupils learn the various points made in the lessons. These are collected in the booklet *Kantu Esperante kun Janico kaj Johano* (*Sing in Esperanto with Janice and John*). A high-quality cassette recording of these songs is available with the booklet.[9] She has even produced a videotape in which some San Diego children teach Esperanto to the viewer. Also available is a videotape about the global education program at H. D. Cooke School in Washington, DC, mentioned above.[10]

A new textbook for children, *Ludu kun Ni (Play with Us)*, by Elisabetta Vilisics Formaggio, has been published recently in Italy.[11] Produced for a project called "Fundapax" (partially funded by UNESCO), the project studies the value of Esperanto in the learning of other languages. Much support for this project is being provided by the "Esperanto" Radikala Asocio of Rome. Schools involved in this project are located in Chad, Germany, Hungary, Italy, the Philippines, Portugal, Spain, the United States, and Zaire.

In 1995 an Esperanto video series based on the BBC's *Muzzy in Gondoland* is to be available.[12] The Muzzy cartoon material has already been used to teach English and other national languages. Now it is being modified for teaching Esperanto to children all over the world. The video uses only Esperanto throughout, and seeks to include the Esperanto ideal that all people of planet Earth are members of the human family.

Those who want to learn more about the research that has been done and is being planned about teaching Esperanto should acquire Alvino E. Fantini and Timothy G. Reagan, *Esperanto and Education: Toward a Research Agenda*.[13] They write:

> The learning of Esperanto has propaedeutic effects with respect to the learning of other languages, and perhaps even other subject matter. In other words, the learning of Esperanto will reduce the time needed for the learning of other languages (and perhaps other subject matter, such as geography, mathematics, etc.) As an investment, in short, learning Esperanto may have significant benefits unrelated to the acquisition of the international language itself. (p. 28)

At that point they cite a long list of references, the complete information for which is listed in their bibliography.

Can language learning and global education be combined? Esperantists are showing how it can be done. Why aren't more teachers making use of this combination?

Notes

[1]Edward Thorndike, "Summary of a Report to the International Auxiliary Language Association" (New York: Division of Psychology, Institute of Educational Research, Teachers College, Columbia University, 1933); J. H. Halloran, "A Four Year Experiment in Esperanto as an Introduction to French," *British Journal of Educational Psychology*, 22 (1952): 200–04; Bruce Sherwood, "The Educational Value of Esperanto Study," in Rüdiger and Vilma Eichholz (eds.), *Esperanto in the Modern World*, 2nd ed. (Bailieboro, Ontario, Canada: Esperanto Press, 1982) 408–10.

[2]Kastora Klubo, Barbara Chmielewska, str. Pulawska 3-11, 02-515 Warsaw, Poland.

[3]Children around the World, 3876 Belmont Ave., San Diego CA 92116, phone (619) 281-0691.

[4]The coordinator is Giorgio Pagano, "Esperanto" Radikala Asocio, Via di Torre Argentina 76, 00186 Rome, Italy. E-mail: E.R.A.@agora.stm.it.

[5]The editor of *Juna Amiko* is Stefan MacGill, Fácán 9/2, H-2030 Érd, Hungary.

[6]For information write to Dorothy Holland, 5140 San Lorenzo Drive, Santa Barbara, CA 93111.

[7]For details write to Gail Martin, 1103 Sharon Court, McLean, VA 22101, or to Sterling Middle School, 201 W. Holly, Sterling, VA 20164. Recent articles about teaching Esperanto to gifted children include:

Glossop, Ronald J. "International Child-to-Child Correspondence Using Esperanto" *Gifted International* 5.1(1988): 81–84.

Quick, Michelle L. "Does Anyone Here Speak Esperanto?" *Gifted Child Today* (May-June 1989): 15–16.

Nelson, Karen C. "The Whys and Hows of Teaching Esperanto to Gifted Students," *Understanding Our Gifted* (November-December 1992): 5.

For another recent article about Esperanto in the context of educating children, see Jim Carnes,"A Global Language? The Amazing Dr. Esperanto," *Teaching Tolerance* 3.1 (1994): 63.

[8]Esperanto League for North America, P.O. Box 1129, El Cerrito, CA 94530.

[9]Available for $7.00 plus $1.50 handling from the Esperanto League for North America.

[10]For details write to Linda Satterthwaite, 400 Taurus Drive, Ft. Washington, MD 20744.

[11]For details write "Esperanto" Radikala Asocio, Via di Torre Argentina 76, 00186 Rome, Italy. E-mail: E.R.A.@agora.stm.it.

[12]The production and distribution of *Muzi en Gondolando* is under the direction of the Internacia Esperanto-Instituto, Riouwstraat 172, 2585 HW The Hague, The Netherlands. Up-to-date information about the availability and cost of the video can be obtained directly from them.

[13] Alvino E. Fantini and Timothy G. Reagan, *Esperanto and Education: Toward a Research Agenda* (Washington, DC: Esperantic Studies Assn, 1992). Contact person for the Esperantic Studies Association is Dr. E. James Lieberman, 3900 Northampton Street, NW, Washington DC 20015, telephone: (202) 362-3963, internet: ejl@gwuvm.gwu.edu.

From Attitudes toward the Foreign to the Development of Children's International Literacy

Kurt E. Müller

Because I write from the perspective of language education in the United States, I am handicapped in trying to address values of language education: in American schools, language is so clearly undervalued it has at times been legislated out of the curriculum. Nevertheless, I wish to describe some essential characteristics of international education in the early stages of schooling, irrespective of location. In the abstract, the desiderata are lofty. An enumeration of a few characteristics of my own national education environment will not only add ballast to otherwise bouyant balloons but will explain shortcomings in meeting standards of interational literacy.

Ronald Glossop, Timothy Reagan, and Karen Case have directed our attention to the early grades in schools. Let us continue our observations at this level in order to consider some counterproposals. Regardless of where they live, children should discover that although all humans may share a range of emotions that include joy, fear, pride, humility, satisfaction, and despair, the cultures we live in shape our perception of these emotions and guide our responses to emotional events in our lives. Thus, the "stiff upper lip" that is so prized as an appropriate response to a setback in Great Britain, is probably totally unbecoming in Haiti or India, where a lack of emotional response is sooner interpreted as an unwelcome detachment from persons and circumstances. Our diverse cultures guide us in different ways to express our experience in visual arts, music, poetic forms, and discursive treatments. If we develop a curiosity about other places and peoples, we will want to visit and learn something about them. But even if we fail to acquire such an interest, our economies have grown so interdependent that our futures are intertwined. In the absence of an innate curiosity, we must be brought to appreciate our connectedness.

Thus, we have a survival need to learn about others, and, in essence, that may be the primary reason we must study other languages and cultures. Although the intent of this essay is not to argue for the importance of languages in the curriculum, for which I would direct readers to works by Müller, Parker, Phillips, and Simon, that feature inheres in much of the following discussion. My thrust here is an exploration of some of the lessons children will learn when exposed to languages early in their school experience.

Respect for Minority Cultures

For societies with a sizable linguistic minority, inclusion of that minority's language as a subject of study confers on the group a measure of respect that may be missing from daily social interaction between groups. Since it is common for minorities to acquire the "power language" of a community while the dominant group may have little interest in the language of the minority, inclusion of the latter's language in elementary schools offers minority families evidence of recognition of their culture by the dominant social group.[1] At the postsecondary level, a number of ethnic groups have sought to raise the standing of their heritage by endowing chairs at prestigious universities to ensure that their language and literature are taught at least somewhere in the U.S.[2] More recently, proposals such as the addition of an African focus, as Reagan and Case mention, are targeting earlier stages of formal education. Such proposals should be welcomed by language teachers for bringing more opportunities for language learning into discussions of school curricula, but they are not without their challenges in developing community support.

Defusing Backlash

Most colleagues in foreign language and literature with whom I have spoken concerning restrictions on the use of languages other than English dismiss attempts to restrict language use as simple bigotry. The point that is lost in educators' perception of much of the public anxiety manifested in responses to high visibility of some ethnic languages concerns the very inclusivity that offering units in Chinese, Ibo, Korean, or Swahili is intended to foster. The resentment of older ethnic groups toward linguistic recognition of more-recent groups is likely based on a lack of recognition of the ethnicity of the older groups. The typical comment of the rapid-Anglicization advocate, "my ancestors had to learn English, why shouldn't the [name of recent ethnic group, or surrogate derogatory epithet]" is not simply bigotry; it may betray a perceived assault against one's identity. If longer-resident (assimilated) ethnic populations are not recognized when newer minorities are, the result should be described less as paranoia than as reversion to a prior exclusivity. In an attempt to foster "inclusivity" for the newer group, failure to recognize the heritage of those assumed already assimilated in fact resurfaces an older rejection and therefore fails to meet the purported goal. This complaint may be described as a matter of "recognized" versus "unrecognized" minorities.

The Inalienable Right to Ethnicity

The typical loss of ethnic language across three generations of immigrants can perhaps be reversed by schooling children in both their home and adoptive languages.[3] All too frequently we hear of either children who will not speak their parents' language out of embarrassment or parents who discard their linguistic heritage in enthusiasm for adopting the dominant language and culture of the new environment. Parents may embrace the new culture and hope to shed the old, but educators contributing to this "language loss" may have others reasons: they may fear that the brain has only so much capacity for language and reason that preservation of the home language inhibits acquisition of the new.[4] In other communities—and other nations—developing literacy in multiple languages is seen as a matter of course. In an essay on bilingual education published in *Teachers College Record*, Margaret Mead writes of:

> the failure of American and most English-speaking peoples to produce high levels of literacy in English when children were taught from the beginning only in English, as compared with the success of the Dutch in the former East Indies who introduced children to literacy in their original languages and produced students who found it easy to become literate in several European languages. (p. 716)

But before we take this fork in the road of inquiry into America's language education, let us define the two prongs of the fork. If we speak in favor of preserving a minority language, as we may infer from the Mead quote, we are allying ourselves with those in ethnic communities who assert a civil right to maintain an ethnic identity within the larger, multiethnic society. It is this civil right that is assaulted when organizations seeking to establish English as the official language of the United States appeal to the public to reject this right as potentially divisive. The assimilation of ethnic groups in America has long had an inherent anglicization component, but the degree to which government policy must force language substitution should be at the heart of any debate on government language policy.

Reagan and Case point out that the English-only advocates imply that those who prefer to speak a language other than English are un-American. In their brochures, these advocates claim they support teaching foreign languages, a claim we may find spurious. In their minimal effort to distinguish between ethnic-language maintenance and "foreign" languages (by either linguistic minorities or anglophones), the English-only agitators point out the other prong of the fork.

Although elementary-school teachers, secondary-school teachers of English and of foreign languages, teachers (at whatever level) of English as a second language (ESL), and bilingual teachers are all engaged in building language competence, they lack a common professional history. If we research the record of advocacy for language competence, we find a curious gap where minority-language preservation should be seen to contribute a significant pool of skills.

Widespread Support for Foreign Languages

If we ask parents or general citizens about teaching "foreign languages" in schools, the overwhelming response is to support inclusion of language study. For example, a survey undertaken by the University of Michigan Survey Research Center in April 1979 asked about public support for language teaching. The respondents, 91.9% of whom were native speakers of English, endorsed language study at all levels, and many considered they might study one or more languages themselves in the future: 93% agreed languages should be offered in secondary school; over 75% thought they should be offered in elementary school; 47% would require language in secondary school; and 40% would require it in elementary school (Eddy). Five years later, a survey in the San Diego area found similar results: 82% of parents thought the school system should offer languages in the elementary school; 46% were willing to pay [extra] for this instruction (Schinke-Llano, p. 33, citing Rickards). Similarly, in response to an exploratory language (FLEX) program initiated in one elementary school near the University of Tennessee, Knoxville, and subsequently expanded to more grades and instruction sites, Patricia Davis Wiley reports an enthusiastic reception by parents and teachers that facilitated the expansion. Importantly,

> Most classroom teachers whose children are participating in the FLEX program consistently comment that their children have become more "Language aware" than non-FLEX children. The same children who rarely volunteer responses in other subjects are those who appear to be more motivated and eager to volunteer in the FLEX classes (p. 55)

If a FLEX program offers a smattering of each language offered in the school district, no one language is favored and the diversity is both welcomed and non-threatening. The results are likely to be less positive if the question in public-support polls asks about specific languages or about schooling linguistic minorities in their own languages. In some communities, some local residents will see Spanish as a threat to the power structure, while others will support it, just as such support for bilingual English-German programs existed in many cities in the mid- to late 19th century. Thus, in San Diego, two-way bilingual programs, in which both English-speaking and Spanish-speaking children are taught in both languages, enjoy popular support. Two-way programs are rare, however.

Additive Bilingualism and Ethnic-Language Development

For all its excellence in advocating a thorough infusion of foreign-language study throughout American education, William Riley Parker's superb volume *The National Interest and Foreign Languages* now strikes me as flawed in possessing a curious gap: silence on language maintenance by ethnic minorities. During the deliberations of the President's Commission on Foreign Language and International Studies, the chairman, James A. Perkins, remarked during the Commission's New York hearing that minority-language preservation had a role to play in meeting the nation's need for individuals with competence in other languages. No other Commission member pursued this thought, so it languished as too far afield from the matter at hand. The Commission's agenda was to bring anglophone Americans to the realization that the nation needed them to acquire competence in an additional language (the "anglophone" qualifier was unspoken, its relevance most likely unappreciated).

Other indications of an inherent underappreciation of ethnic resources—if not outright racist prejudice—can be found in the record of American education and of academe's professional organizations. Prior to the late 1960s, when foreign languages were a widespread requirement in secondary schools in preparation for admission to colleges, what was the experience of children from ethnic minorities? Could they use their home language in fulfillment of this requirement? My experience in testing ethnic speakers who have not formally studied their language is that their domain of language experience is often limited to family activities to such an extent that they demonstrate insufficient proficiency through such instruments as the [U.S. Department of] Defense Language Proficiency Test. Given the impediment of limited domain, were they encouraged to study their ethnic language to develop competence in it? Or were they sooner directed to study another language, or none at all?[5]

Myopia in Vocational Education, or, Anti-Intellectual Education Undermines Peace and National Security

The collusion of academic associations in undermining language study is seen more clearly through the prism of hindsight. Parker, who was executive secretary of the Modern Language Association of America (MLA), points out the publication by the National Education Association's Educational Policies Commission of *Education for All American Youth*, a volume that promoted a curriculum we might describe as narrowly vocational in that it suggested literature, foreign languages, and chemistry are among "peripheral subjects" that some students might elect in their free time. Parker mentions as well a curriculum recommended by twelve Harvard authors and 60 consultants, *General Education in a Free Society*, from which languages were omitted.

Recognition of Additive Bilingualism among Anglophones

Several of the reports Parker criticizes are clearly a product of their time. Written during World War II, published either during or immediately after the war, or undertaken in the immediate postwar period, they betray an isolationist attitude as well as anti-intellectual bias.

But the MLA itself betrays the influence of war hysteria. In his review of contributions by association members to the Allied effort in World War II, Percy W. Long notes that many senior members of Allied organizations were MLA members. He briefly glosses over the deprivation of civil liberties of some MLA members who were interned during the war.

Detached from any perception of an internal security threat, we can look back on this episode and note that the education lesson of 50 years ago was clearly that mainstream Americans, i.e., those not identifiable with an ethnic background (especially a suspect one), needed competence in other languages.[6]

Arguments for "additive bilingualism" have received better reception from school boards than have proposals for language maintenance.[7] Arguments in favor of acquiring an additional language are also consonant with other long-term education philosophies: lifelong learning, global or international education, and traditional liberal-arts curricula. The anti-foreigner attitude may combine with a counter-productive anti-elitist bias to undermine the development of a national personnel resource of individuals skilled in, or even conversant with, other languages.

Elitism and Countercurrents in Australian Education

The United States is not the only country to encounter an anti-intellectual bias in education policy that hinders the development of personnel skills. In *Issues in Second Language and Cross-Cultural Education: The Forest through the Trees*, Gail L. Nemetz Robinson notes the impact of elitism on language enrollments in Australian schools, specifically those of the state of New South Wales. Robinson traces the elitist roots of attitudes toward language education to remarks made in 1935 by the assistant undersecretary of the New South Wales department of education, who "recommended that an intelligence quotient of 120 be required for the study of more than one language" (p. 91). According to Robinson, the result in the 1970s is that

> The weighted mean IQ of the combined French and German candidates at the S.C.E. [School Certificate Exam] in 1971 was 118.45, compared to 109.58 for the English candidates [i.e., those who had not studied French or German, the two languages with the highest enrollments]. The weighted mean IQ of the combined French and German candidates at the H.S.C.E. [Higher School Certificate Exam] in 1972 was 120.45, compared with 115.90 for the English candidates.

The negative impact of this elitist channeling of only gifted students into languages resulted in a decline in enrollments. As Robinson explains,

> In an attempt to change the elitist position of foreign language study, which had continued through the years, and to remove the discrimination of the extant "two language, one language, no language" streams of study, the Wyndham Scheme [an education reform] made all foreign language study an elective in 1963.... It is no wonder that a subject whose potentially successful learners were thought to require an average IQ of 120 was excluded from the core of the curriculum. Few educators could, in all good conscience, willfully subject the majority of the general student population to certain failure (pp. 91–92).

The Socioeconomically Disadvantaged

More-recent advocates of early language learning have begun to emphasize the educational achievement of underprivileged groups that are given the opportunity to acquire an additional language. In an urban school district that demonstrates a racial distribution of 57% black and 43% white, with 52% of the district population receiving free or reduced-cost lunches through a government program, one does not expect to find a socioeconomically advantageous environment for educational attainment. But Carolyn Andrade reports that of students in Cincinnati's language magnet program over a six-year period, 61.2%–72.3% scored at or above the 50th percentile in reading; 59.9%–77.7% did so in mathematics. For the above-average stanine range, for which a normal distribution would be 23% of the population, the results for children in the foreign language program ranged from a low of 23.7% (one year's results) to a high of 37.5% in reading; math-score distribution ranged for this period from 21.3% to 40.8% of the students scoring in the upper stanine range.

In this volume, Helene Zimmer-Loew reports on the trans-European initiatives of the Council of Europe. Of particular interest is the Council's orientation toward fostering acquisition of languages through a spectrum of societal organizations, i.e., in formal education; in informal, community environments; and through home-based technology. Not only is language to be learned throughout schools and universities, but also through channels of vocational education. Of course travel by journeymen is nothing new to the guild system, but the emphasis on experience in three different countries in addition to one's own is a particularly notable innovation that should be emulated elsewhere.

By comparison with all the other industrialized nations, language education in the U.S. is sorely lacking. In a study of fifteen countries, two thirds had a foreign language requirement of eight or more years. The anglophone countries England and Scotland had the shortest foreign language requirement, three and four years respectively (though England was to add two more years in 1995), and three nations' schools had required sequences of at least ten years (Bergentoft, fig. 1, pp. 22–23). Although Japan has no requirement as such, 98% of Japanese study another language (p. 29).

In light of such comparisons, I take issue not with the specifics of the Glossop and Reagan and Case papers, but with their capitulation to certain forces in American society. Beginning in the quarter-century prior to World War I, some political groups launched efforts to thwart the teaching of languages other than English, and such opposition has kept language education in America from reclaiming the position it once held. The thrust of the argument by Reagan and Case is properly oriented toward students that are not now engaged in language study, but they propose alternatives to foreign language study for all children. I believe there is no alternative. The schools are remiss to avoid essential elements of education. If we accept the substitution of a sampling of language experiences for sequential acquisition of a foreign language, we undermine attempts to meet our national need for individuals capable of using other languages. Until we achieve a curriculum that enables students to discuss global issues through the medium of another language, we will not be internationally literate.

Does Study of a European Language Imply Eurocentrism?

Glossop would substitute Esperanto for natural languages as the logical choice when confronted with the difficult question: Which language should children study when we cannot predict the language(s) they will require later in life (if any at all, some would add)? I answer the question with "any of several world languages or a language of specific relevance to the child." Glossop's point cannot be overemphasized that omitting a language component from global education is tantamount to teaching children "*they do not need to learn any other language*" (his emphasis) and that such an omission is inimical to the goals of global education. And for anglophones Esperanto is likely to be the global language *par excellence*. Glossop indicates numerous organizations and materials to facilitate global correspondence to address issues typical of global education. But let us not overlook the potential contribution to global education of natural languages. French teachers, in particular, have become aware of the need to add to their materials on French culture so as to be concerned with francophone culture, e.g., Acadian, African, and Québecois. I have used my own limited French to speak with Haitians and Zaïrians and, in delivering services to Kurdish refugees, with francophone Europeans in Southwest Asia. Médicins sans frontières (Doctors without Borders), a Nobel-Peace-Prize-winning organization, is also known by its Dutch name, Artsen zonder Grenzen, as some of its members originate from Holland. Consequently, one can see where Dutch can offer access to refugee issues, not to mention material on Caribbean or East Asian islands with Dutch colonial connections. I have used German in Africa, Asia, and the Caribbean, primarily dealing with public-health and human-rights issues among refugees. European members of international and charitable organizations that send volunteers to the third world offer excellent opportunities to speak German with individuals whose experience is in global or third-world issues. The American Association of Teachers of German devoted an issue of its pedagogical journal to racial diversity in reaching students and multicultural material supporting the teaching of German (for Afro-German issues in particular, see Hopkins). At slightly later grade levels than our emphasis here, there are also examples of using German to acquire information on emerging and third-world countries. Tenth-grade students of German in Ephrata (Pennsylvania) High School have corresponded with their peers learning German in a high school in Riga, Latvia, and ninth-graders have received correspondence in German from university students in Hohhot, Inner Mongolia, and Beijing, China (Anderson).[8]

With such examples, one sees that European languages are no more restricted to European issues than is English restricted to North America and the British Isles. As a means of information on the third world, European languages can indeed be useful. While it is thus possible to use second languages to explore third cultures, it is not typical. In their professional preparation, language teachers are taught about the cultures of those nations that use the target language as their official language. From this perspective, those teachers interested in offering Esperanto may be more likely to demonstrate kindred spirits with the goals of global education than are most elementary school teachers with enough credits in a language to qualify as elementary-school foreign language teachers. This constraint can be redressed through professional development activities such as in-service workshops (Rosenbusch).

Language Arts and Opportunity Cost

Reagan and Case suggest that children can learn about languages spoken around the world, language families, language change, and the development of English. Certainly, the confluence of themes in history, geography, and language arts would allow for mutual reinforcement. If implemented in early grades, such an approach would put a welcome end to the education fraud perpetrated across the United States under the name of "language arts." (Until such time as the concept of language arts attains a comparative dimension, it should be grouped with such obscenities as the claim by English-only advocates that they favor learning foreign languages.) But at what grade should this teaching begin? If such culinary sampling is a predecessor to actual language learning, we incur an opportunity cost in actual language development. I hesitate to accept any proposal that postpones a meaningful encounter with a language through repeated use and development, parallel to the student's experience with English. If we accept the need to start language study early so as to foster the development of good accents, acquire literacy in the second language, and use it as a means of acquiring knowledge rather than as solely an object of study, we cannot in good conscience postpone the sequence of study beyond elementary school.

In effect, my quarrel with Reagan and Case is capable of resolution by adopting their suggestions within a more-expansionist concept of language arts. In suggesting "linguistics for kids," they point the way to end the fraud. Their suggestions should not be adopted as a politically acceptable substitute for learning another language but should be considered in the context of broadening language experience. As will become clear in the next section of this essay, language experience in formal education (distinct from the longer sequence of experience needed for meaningful language acquisition) is most appropriate in middle- and junior-high-school curricula. The Glossop and Reagan and Case proposals are certainly germane to exploratory language courses, but exploratory courses and the 6th–8th-grade curriculum should be used to broaden experience already encountered; they should not be an excuse to postpone second language acquisition.

Characteristics of Children's Language Learning

School districts may resist instituting language programs in the early grades or cut them because they add to faculty costs, but that does not necessarily indicate a lack of parental support. Weak programs that are not coordinated with later language study ("articulated" in the professional jargon), that fail to address faculty recruiting and professional development, that are not integrated with other classroom activities, or that do not clearly state instructional goals and therefore cannot be shown to meet them will not engender a degree of parental support sufficient to confront a school board considering dropping an early language program. Those that do meet these criteria can muster unusual community interest. When Glastonbury, Connecticut, tried to eliminate its FLES program, a combination of parents and realtors flexed some political muscle to reinstate the program. In fact, parental support for early language programs, particularly early immersion programs,[9] is so strong that an organization of parents in Canada and the United States has grown to support such initiatives.[10]

Myriam Chapman, Elizabeth Grob, and Mari Haas have presented an overview of the characteristics of children's language learning at various ages from nursery school to early adolescence. If we look at some of these characteristics, we see how appropriate it is to teach additional languages to children as early as nursery school.

> Four and five year olds delight in language. They are internalizing new vocabulary, through visual images, physical experience, and concrete examples. While they are still working on their own language development, they are eager to learn new words in other languages as well. (p. 28)

> Six-seven is a transitional age.... Children at this age are conceptualizing more. They have more experiences to build on and are able to think about them.... the foreign language teacher needs to plan many concrete experiences from which children can conceptualize, thereby challenging their thinking skills.... [The language teacher can include] games and folk dances that require more complicated and challenging movements. (p. 30)

In first and second grade, children's awareness of community develops, and the elementary-school curriculum reflects this expanding sense of environment. If games and folk dances are included in the curriculum, they can easily be taught through another language. In this manner, children become aware of different cultures through the medium of another language. With regard to their ability to manipulate scissors and paper or draw more accurately than at earlier ages, children can engage in mapmaking at this age. But Chapman, Grob, and Haas remind us

> maps of the United States or the world are still mysterious to them.... remember that children who can sound terrifically

knowledgeable when talking about where they have been on vacation or where grandma lives, do not really have a sense of geography. (p. 32)

For eight, nine, and ten year olds, experience with another language reinforces their own exploration of language niceties, gaps, and oddities. "[T]hey love codes (spoken and written), made-up languages, puns, rhymes, and other revisions of their everyday symbols" (p. 33). Thus, we understand the fascination experienced by the young Blaise Pascal, the 17th-century philosopher and mathematician, when his father taught him a secret language for their private communication. When he discovered that others knew this language also and that books had been published in it, his father confided he'd taught him classical Greek (Marshall).

Wallace Lambert and Otto Klineberg have found that ten year olds are more receptive than fourteen year olds to people of different backgrounds, so it is reasonable to set the stage for appreciation of foreign cultures even earlier. If children in the 8–10 age group experience facets of another culture through another language, they accept it without prejudice. As their own self-concept is developing at this age along with both more objectivity and judgmental evaluations, children with exposure to additional languages can already apply more than one perspective to how they see others. As Chapman, Grob, and Haas see it, at this age they can "take a look behind the sometimes oppressive labels placed on people of other cultures" (p. 34).

As children emerge from elementary to middle and junior high school, they encounter a change in the orientation of teaching. Subject matter is presented in isolation by different teachers, and children are expected to be capable of abstraction. Anne Nerenz examines various developmental observations for the eleven-to-fourteen-year age group and concludes tentatively

- that the middle years are a time for maturation of cognitive skills already initiated and learned rather than the acquisition of new skills.
- that the school curriculum overestimates the number of students who are capable of formal operations and abstract thinking
- that instruction during this period should "avoid the introduction of new cognitive skills and include a much larger component of experience and practice of skills already acquired in the cognitive area" ...

- that the curriculum should "include a large component of experience and practice of skills within opportunities for interaction with nature, society and people"...

Following these observations, one may conclude that this is the wrong age to introduce a language via grammatical instruction, or that it is appropriate only for those children whose ability to deal with abstractions has already developed sufficiently. Yet it is at this age that many language programs are first offered and that, in the U.S., children are taught grammar in their first language.[11]

Given the discussion above, a grammatical approach to Esperanto should not occur earlier than junior high school. Alternatively, if Esperanto is taught with the methods used for most modern languages in elementary-school programs, emphasizing concrete language use, then an elementary-school experience with Esperanto could be background for treatment in junior high school of language structure. In a FLEX offering, thought must be given to the inclusiveness of languages represented. If languages are chosen from those offered at the next level, all should be included. If chosen to represent minority groups in the community, representation of several groups is appropriate. One of the ironies of the circumstances surrounding our discussion is that Ludwig Zamenhof invented Esperanto as a neutral language of communication, devoid of the associations with the relative economic, diplomatic, or military power of the national languages one encounters in international discourse; yet, as Reagan and Case point out, groups may object to teaching Esperanto because of its "internationalist" intent.[12]

In the past, some have advocated limiting the languages available for study to those with generally appreciated literature or those of specific scientific importance. I suspect this argument presented by many German-Americans in the late 19th century may have contributed to the backlash against widespread teaching of (and in) German that began in the late 1880s. Therefore, some circumspection about offering multiple languages and recognizing many is important to avoid the perception that some groups are offered disproportionate deference while others are ignored. Lest we repeat this experience at the turn of the 20th to the 21st century with regard to Spanish, school systems should ensure that Spanish is offered along with a choice of other languages so as not to antagonize support for all language teaching by forcing schooling in only one second language.

If, in support of local minorities, languages are to be offered for which there is a shortage of qualified teachers, it is likely that schools will want to turn to community resources outside the education sector. If volunteers are used to introduce children to such languages, these recommendations by Gladys Lipton are in order:

> Adult volunteers (parents and members of the community) may be used..., but it must be remembered that there must be training sessions for these volunteers. Knowledge of and proficiency in the foreign language is not enough. Volunteers want and need training in classroom management, sequencing and pacing of lessons, lesson planning, planning effective and varied lessons, evaluating progress, reviewing and reinforcing concepts, etc. (p. 48)

If volunteers are only available when their children are in the grade(s) at which this program operates, coordinators must develop additional resources, perhaps ensuring representation of different languages at different times.

Throughout elementary and secondary education in the United States, the choice of additional languages is extremely limited. At the postsecondary level, the choice of languages available for study is actually quite broad: Brod and Huber identified 125 languages offered in American institutions of higher education in 1990. Can some of this variety make its way to earlier grades? If so, how widespread can language choice become?

The difficulty with offering many languages in a school system lies in accruing a critical mass of students that will pursue study of the language for several years. This requirement is sometimes difficult to meet even in commonly taught languages, particularly if pressures of conformity channel students into certain high-density languages. In communities with scores of minorities, an offering of sequential language study in all languages spoken in the community would be unworkable, but units of study or elements of experience in these languages would be highly relevant to an exploratory language course or a true language-arts course. In this instance, elements from various languages spoken in the community can enrich a language arts program through examples of similar greetings or other phrases across languages in the same family, samples of varying writing systems, attention to tonal inflections or forms of address in some languages, and correspondence between oral speech and written representation. If children at the middle- or junior-high-school level are presented with material concerning diverse means of communication, the multiplicity of writing systems would be a natural ingredient to any exploration that might include semaphore flags, Morse code, sign language, and artistic expression.

But acquisition of international literacy—knowledge of world issues as well as the means to share one's information, emotions, and experiences with others—requires attention to sustained sequential language instruction. We can neither limit our language experience to oral discourse within a limited domain nor promote the acquisition of another language within the context of one national culture. If we do, we fail to reach the goal of literacy. And literacy is the primary goal of education.

Notes

[1] Similar circumstances obtain for societies that have dominant languages or dialects spoken by a minority in that the group that speaks the dominant language/dialect is likely to have little interest in the idiom of the masses. The obvious contrast with the situation described in the text is that in representative democracies one expects the power language to be the language of the majority whereas a minority that speaks a power language is assumed to be characteristic of undemocratic societies. A digression: In this regard, it will be interesting to observe whether the recently installed government of Jean-Bertrand Aristide, elected with 67% of the vote, will take steps to raise the status of Creole within Haitian society. Although Creole is now recognized, my experience working with refugee Haitian teachers demonstrates a great degree of discomfort regarding their ability to teach a standard Creole; they are far more comfortable remaining with French. In a country with an 80% illiteracy rate, avoidance of teaching the language Haitians are most familiar with seems counterproductive and may well contribute to maintain social distinctions that would inhibit upward mobility.

[2] Not all academics, even in language and literature, recognize the value of some esoteric cultures: I've heard one such position described by a renowned professor of English as a "rug chair."

[3] On language maintenance by immigrants and their offspring, see Fishman. On the claim that current immigrant populations are losing their native tongue in the second generation, see Crawford.

[4]See, e.g., D.J. Saer, "The Effect of Bilingualism on Intelligence," *British Journal of Psychology* 14 (1923): 35–38, who found that Welsh children who conducted most activities in Welsh but were schooled in English performed poorly on intelligence tests. Flaws to look for in such studies are an absence of identified social factors such as class or socioeconomic status of the subjects, prestige or dominant language in the society and prevalent attitudes toward the language of the subjects, and whether literacy is developed in one or more languages.

[5]By the mid-1970s, during a New York City fiscal crisis, the reverse perception of education administrators had taken hold. In attempts to trim the budget of the City University, proposals were put forth to teach some languages at some campuses, others at other locations, with the assumption that campuses with large ethnic-minority enrollments would offer the language of that ethnic group. Given the agitation among ethnic Hispanics for recognition of civil rights, this solution is comprehensible. But it also betrays a set of prejudices, such as assuming that Hispanics wouldn't want to learn German, for example, or, worse, aren't capable of doing so. As an example to the contrary, for public-school programs in Chinese in Springfield, Massachusetts (grades 7–12), children whose first language is Spanish are enrolled in Chinese in every school that offers it (conversation with Kathleen Riordan, Springfield Public Schools, 8 April 1995). We must also recognize that teaching a "heritage" language to a member of a specific ethnic group is not necessarily easy. If a dialect of the language is spoken at home or if the family members who speak the language are not schooled in it, the linguistic-minority child may have all the challenges of anglophone children plus a few more.

[6]We need to recognize that native-born U.S. citizens whose ancestral cultures were wartime enemies may have been the most likely candidates for training in these languages. The Nisei are the first to come to mind. Americans of Japanese Ancestry (AJA), the U.S. Army trained them to develop literacy in a language the public schools would not have dreamed to promote. N.B., the term AJA was frequently used along with ACA (Chinese) and AAA (Asian) and demonstrates the race-consciousness of the era. While race conscious, army leaders directing the efforts of the Nisei appear to have defended them against any public suspicion of disloyalty.

[7]On legislation restricting the use of languages of out-of-favor ethnic groups, see Leibowitz.

[8]Personal communication with Mara Anderson, Ephrata, PA, School District, 8 April 1995. Prospective teachers of English at the universities in Beijing and Hohhot are required to study German as an additional language. Ms. Anderson harnessed this piece of information on a trip to Inner Mongolia and used it to generate correspondence with her students in Pennsylvania.

[9]Early immersion programs typically conduct their instruction entirely in a language foreign to the students' home language and add the language of

the community incrementally over the next few years until instruction is approximately equally divided between the two languages.

[10] Advocates for Language Learning, P.O. Box 4964, Culver City, CA 90230.

[11] One wonders whether the legacy of World-War-I-era legislation outlawing the teaching of languages other than English generally and in elementary schools in particular had the multiple purpose of bigotry against specific ethnic groups, restriction of language learning to the academic elite (high schools at that time were all preparatory schools for higher education; they were not generally attended by all), and avoidance of the possibility that younger pupils might see foreigners in a positive light.

[12] On the "subversive" reputation of Esperanto, see Lins and, accessible in a previous volume in this series, Tonkin.

Works Cited

Andrade, Carolyn, Richard R. Kretschmer, Jr., and Laura W. Kretschmer. "Two Languages for All Children: Expanding to Low Achievers and the Handicapped." In *Languages in Elementary Schools*. Ed. Kurt E. Müller. New York: American Forum, 1989. 177–203.

Brod, Richard [I]., and Bettina J. Huber. "Foreign Language Enrollments in United States Institutions of Higher Education, Fall 1990." *ADFL Bulletin* 23.3 (1992): 6–10.

Crawford, James. *Hold Your Tongue: Bilingualism and the Politics of "English Only."* Reading, MA: Addison-Wesley, 1992.

Eddy, Peter A. "Foreign Languages in the USA: A National Survey of American Attitudes and Experience." In *President's Commission on Foreign Language and International Studies: Background Papers and Studies*. James A. Perkins, chairman. Washington, DC: GPO, 1979. 78–80. rpt. with expanded detail as "Attitudes toward Foreign Language Study and Requirements in American Schools and Colleges: Results of a National Survey." *ADFL Bulletin* 11.2 (1979): 4–9.

Fishman, Joshua A. *Language Loyalty in the United States: The Maintenance and Perpetuation of Non-English Mother Tongues by American Ethnic and Religious Groups*. The Hague: Mouton, 1966.

Hopkins, Leroy T., Jr. "Expanding the Canon: Afro-German Studies." *Die Unterrichtspraxis* 25.2 (1992): 121–26.

Lambert, Wallace E., and Otto Klineberg. *Children's Views of Foreign Peoples*. New York: Meredith, 1967.

Leibowitz, Arnold H. "Language and the Law: The Exercise of Political Power through Official Designation of Language." In *Language and Politics*. Ed. William M. O'Barr and Jean F. O'Barr. The Hague: Mouton, 1976. 213–34.

Lins, Ulrich. *Die gefährliche Sprache*. Gerlingen: Bleicher,1988.

Long, Percy W. "The Modern Language Association of America in World War II." *PMLA: Proceedings* 64 (1948): 66–68; 70.

Marshall, Donald G. "Mother Tongue and Father Grammar, or, Why Should Children Learn a Second Language." In *Languages in Elementary Schools*. Ed. Kurt E. Müller. New York: American Forum, 1989. 157–76.

Mead, Margaret. "The Conservation of Insight—Educational Understanding of Bilingualism." *Teachers College Record* 79.4 (1978): 705–21.

Müller, Kurt E. *Language Competence: Implications for National Security*. New York: Praeger, 1986. Center for Strategic and International Studies. Washington Papers Series 119.

Nerenz, Anne G. "The Exploratory Years: Foreign Languages in the Middle-Level Curriculum." In *Shifting the Instructional Focus to the Learner*. Ed. Sally Sieloff Magnan. Middlebury, VT: Northeast Conference, 1990. 93–126. NEC is currently at 29 Ethan Allen Drive, Colchester, VT 05446, but will move to central Pennsylvania in late 1995.

Parker, William Riley. *The National Interest and Foreign Languages*. 3d ed. Washington, DC: GPO, 1962.

Phillips, June K., comp. *New Cases for Foreign Language Study*. Middlebury, VT: Northeast Conference, 1981.

Rickards, G.E. "Parental Attitude in the San Diego Area regarding Foreign Language Study at the Elementary School Level." Diss. US International University. *DAI* 45/05A, 1262-A. ED 245 532.

Rosenbusch, Marcia H. "Is Knowledge of Cultural Diversity Enough? Global Education in the Elementary School Foreign Language Program." *Foreign Language Annals* 25.2 (1992): 129–36.

Schinke-Llano, Linda. *Foreign Language in the Elementary School: State of the Art*. Washington, DC: Center for Applied Linguistics ERIC Clearinghouse on Languages and Linguistics, 1985. Language in Education: Theory and Practice Series.

Simon, Paul. *The Tongue-Tied American: Confronting the Foreign Language Crisis*. New York: Continuum, 1980.

Tonkin, Humphrey. "Esperanto in Eastern Europe: An Insurmountable Opportunity?" In *Language as Barrier and Bridge*. Ed. Kurt E. Müller. Papers of the Center for Research and Documentation on World Language Problems 2. Lanham, MD: University Press of America, 1992. 59–65.

Wiley, Patricia Davis. "A Model Foreign Language Experience Program for the Elementary School." In *Children and Languages: Research, Practice, and Rationale for the Early Grades*. Comp. Rosemarie Benya and Ed. Kurt E. Müller. (New York: National Council on Foreign Language and International Studies, 1988). 51–58.

A Brief Response to Kurt Müller

Ronald J. Glossop

On page 125 of "From Attitudes toward the Foreign to the Development of Children's International Literacy" Kurt Müller says, "In the light of such comparisons [between the United States and other countries with regard to the amount of time devoted to foreign language instruction], I take issue not with the specifics of the Glossop and Reagan and Case papers, but with their capitulation to certain forces in American society." I suppose that the reference here is to those forces in American society that think everybody in the world is going to use English. I certainly am *not* capitulating to those forces. In fact, I am arguing *against* those forces. Rather than being influenced by any forces within the United States, I am responding to general forces within the *global society*, the change from inter-nationalism to globalism. The world is changing from a globe where the different nation-states could be represented in different colors with definite borders to one like the photo of Earth from space where there are no national borders and where it is evident that we are all members of a planetary community. Inter-nationalism means still focusing on those nation-states and their governments and the national languages they like to promote. Globalism means having a single, neutral second language for everyone on Earth, so that we can all communicate with each other without some people having the unfair advantage of using their own national language.

In the section entitled "Does Study of a European Language Imply Eurocentrism?" Müller seems to miss the central point I was making about being able to use Esperanto to communicate throughout the global community and not just with certain countries or regions of the world. Müller is certainly correct in noting that natural European languages may be used in some places outside Europe, but my point is that those languages are still national languages and are used only in certain geographical areas. The thrust of my argument is not against a European focus but rather against an *inter-national* orientation with a focus on national languages and national cultures instead of a *global* orientation, which views the whole planet as one community.

Indeed one argument sometimes advanced against Esperanto is that it is a European language, but from its beginning over 100 years ago it has had a global focus. Its aim has always been to serve the world community, not just Europe. The fact is that cultures throughout the world community have been influenced by Europe and European languages. Mandarin Chinese may be spoken by more people than any other language, but the most widely used international languages are English, French, and Spanish. If you could mix those three languages together in a blender and then strain the resulting mixture through a filter that would transmit only those components that are consistent with a few basic rules, you would have something very much like Esperanto. Thus throughout the world, most pupils would find something in Esperanto that is already familiar to them. It would also be a completely phonetic language so that one could move freely between the written and spoken forms of the language. With regard to the suitability of Esperanto for Asians and others not already familiar with European languages, I would argue that those people still can learn Esperanto much more rapidly than any other European national language. Furthermore, the experience will not carry the taint of cultural imperialism that the national languages do. People have learned Esperanto because its ideal of human unity-with-diversity has appealed to them, not because they were forced to learn it.

That brings me to another point, which Müller sweems to ignore completely, even though it was one of my central points. Esperanto is in a class by itself because of how quickly children can learn it. It can be used after only a short period of time rather than requiring students to study a language for a couple of years before they can really start using it. Esperanto is totally phonetic. It is totally rule-guided even to the point of always being accented on the next-to-last syllable. Consequently, children can start using it rather quickly. The result is quick, positive reinforcement with regard to learning a new language, something that will not happen with any national language. At the same time, students will be given the confidence to tackle that next language, and what they have learned while studying Esperanto will help them to do that.

Müller's point on page 131 that "a grammatical approach to Esperanto should not occur earlier than junior high school" is not supported by his own quotations. He notes on page 130 that eight, nine, and ten year olds "love codes (spoken and written), made-up languages" and so on. Well, Esperanto *is* a code for them. It is a made-up language. Müller seems to think that learning grammar must wait until later because it necessarily involves abstract thinking, but in Esperanto learning the grammar is a concrete part of learning the language. The grammar coding of Esperanto makes learning gramatical terms such as "noun," "adjective," "verb," "preposition," and "direct object" a part of learning the language. I know from personal experience that fifth graders can learn about grammar from studying Esperanto and that it helps them understand English grammar. We should think of Esperanto as a modern, streamlined Latin. It does everything that the study of Latin once did for high school students with the important difference of eliminating a great deal of unhelpful memorization of genders and multiple conjugations and declensions and irregular forms. As a result it can be taught in elementary school and engenders a positive attitude rather than a negative one (as Latin often did) toward the subsequent study of other new languages.

In the next-to-last paragraph Müller says, "If chldren at the middle- or junior-high-school level are presented with material concerning diverse means of communication, the multiplicity of writing systems would be a natural ingredient to any exploration that might include semaphore flags, Morse code, sign language, and artistic expression." That seems a good idea to me, but why not also include some international communication via computer or mail with other young people throughout the world using the Esperanto that they learned in the fifth and sixth grades?

Language Equality at the United Nations: An Achievable Dream

Humphrey Tonkin

The first step in resolving the language problems of the United Nations is recognizing that the organization has them. Some people claim that the present six-language system works well, and they are disinclined to disturb procedures that have in recent years remained remarkably free from controversy.

But we must be clear about the function and purpose of the UN's policy of multilingualism, which may be different from the public statements on the matter. Certainly, if we believe that it is intended to facilitate communication among the member-states, we must recognize that a great deal of the energy expended by the interpreting and translating staff is wasted effort. For the most part, delegates and officials working in New York are speakers of English. Their command of the language may vary, especially in some of the smaller missions of member-states, but few are without any knowledge of English at all. Many of them rely heavily on translation and interpretation into English, both to provide them with linguistic material that they can understand and, in many cases, to convert speeches or texts from their own languages into English, the primary language of international currency.

Thus, interpretation and translation into English is an important element in advancing communication. In the corridors of the building on the East River, it is generally English that provides a linguistic meeting place for the delegates. The old imperial languages, especially French and Spanish and to a lesser extent Russian, may be used in encounters of the inheritors of these linguistic legacies, just as Arabic serves among delegates of at least some of the Arab states. But when delegates of varied backgrounds meet, it is English that they tend to use. (On the distinction between informal and formal language use at the UN, see Jastrab, 1984.)

While there are exceptions, the other language services are no longer intended primarily as facilitators of communication, if they were ever so intended, but as political symbols. By insisting on the language rights of French or Spanish or Arabic speakers, the member-states for whom these are native languages are accorded the political recognition *de jure* that allows them to accept the role of English as lingua franca *de facto*. Obtaining and maintaining official status for one's language at the United Nations is a sign of international status and prestige. In some sense, the very lack of utility of services in a given language shows that the owners of that language have the power to impose their will on others.

If enough governments are empowered to use their languages officially, the remaining have-nots, possessors for the most part of languages of limited utility beyond their own borders, are in no position to overturn the existing procedures. Even the have-nots can take comfort from the fact that the hegemony of the United States and its English-speaking friends is not wholly reflected in the official language structure. In other words, they too have something of a vested interest in the status quo. If they challenge the weaker official languages, they may only reinforce the position of English.

This is not to say that language services in the five languages other than English remain unused or neglected. They help develop terminology for those member-states for whom these languages are native, and they offer a regular flow of documentation that can be used by these member-states in communication with their governments and in numerous other ways. Thus they perform valuable services for certain privileged member-states. What they mostly do not do is provide cost-effective services to those member-states for whom the languages in question are not the official languages of government.

My analysis is of course oversimplified and a more sophisticated observer might add refinements and modifications to it, but it is remarkable how few people cut through the rhetoric to recognize the political dimension in the current language regime at the UN. The solutions that they suggest tend to be directed towards solving a problem that exists only to a limited degree: they seek to improve linguistic understanding, assuming that that is the goal of the language services. Those services are in truth intended less to facilitate communication or improve language equality, than *to set the terms of communication* and *to perpetuate a language inequality roughly parallel to the inequality of actual political power* embodied in the relative standing of the members of the organization. Like dedicated parking-spaces, they set certain delegations apart from the others.

Among those who argue for a change in the language regime at the United Nations is one group that has remained both vocal and marginalized: the advocates of Esperanto. They base their arguments on two claims—first, that the present regime is inefficient and expensive, and, second, that it is based on inequality. The first of these arguments dominated their advocacy of Esperanto at least until the 1960s and 1970s. They maintained that the current system of translation and interpretation was expensive and time-consuming, that it led to misunderstandings, and that delegates were frustrated in their efforts to communicate with one another. But this vision of Babel at Turtle Bay is now outdated, and may never have had much validity. Language differences are often exploited for diplomatic purposes; ambiguity sometimes helps resolve disputes; and in any case direct communication can always be conducted in English.

The failure of the Esperanto advocates' argument to address the salient issues is unfortunate, because the practical claims of Esperanto are considerable. Behind what is sometimes dismissed as mere naive idealism stands an extensive movement of Esperanto speakers (see Janton, 1993). Successfully communicating within their own linguistic envelope, these users of Esperanto are in some sense isolated by a version of the very language barrier they seek to overcome. In part because it uses a different language, their community is little understood, little recognized, and little attended to, but remarkably vigorous and durable. They speak a language that first saw the light of day in 1887, the work of a young Jewish idealist named Lazar Ludwik Zamenhof, who wrote under the pseudonym Doktoro "Esperanto"—"one who hopes." Zamenhof, who witnessed firsthand the corrosive and violent effects of ethnic differences in the Russian empire into which he was born, and moved by universalist sentiments perhaps arising out of the assimilationist Judaism that he inherited, believed that the first step to overcoming ethnic differences was the ability to communicate.

The language that Zamenhof created for this purpose has been called by some a simplified Latin—a Latin of the people perhaps intended to perform for all humankind a similar role to the Yiddish that united Jews in much of Eastern and Central Europe. Had it come into being after, rather than before, Saussure, it would surely have been labelled structuralist in inspiration, for Zamenhof was not confined to the grammatical labels of Latin and the other languages he knew, seeing his language as a language of discrete elements capable of assembly in a multiplicity of ways to convey meaning.

But Zamenhof was not so naive as to imagine that a common language, no matter how ingenious, would solve the problems of the world. It has been pointed out frequently that in a world where everyone is perfectly understood, differences of intent and conflicting goals are all the more apparent. Zamenhof went further: he in effect freely yielded leadership over the early community of speakers of the language, creating thereby a free-standing speech community that could look to him only for the most indirect guidance. He never held office in any Esperanto organization.

He was at great pains to provide this burgeoning community not only with a common sense of purpose but also with a common sense of history, correctly understanding that all new communities need a history that tells them they are *not* new. He translated literary works into Esperanto; he invented proverbs for Esperanto speakers to use; he encouraged the creation of a periodical press and of local organizations. He also created what might be described as an ideology of Esperantism. Though resisted by many, who saw the language as the scientific choice of rational intellectuals, this ideology helped hold the Esperanto movement together through schisms and reform proposals and ultimately through two world wars.

Over the years, hundreds of thousands of people have learned Esperanto, and large numbers of people today have at least a passive knowledge of the language. Its activist core remains more or less constant in size, and it supports a hundred or more regularly published periodicals, a steady stream of original and translated literature (perhaps two hundred volumes a year), broadcasts from a dozen or so radio stations around the world, and an annual World Congress that brings together on average some 2500 people. Esperanto is a language of the underground, flourishing in environments of political oppression, and opening up opportunities for international communication that exist in part because of its very obscurity. Thus the speakers of the language have something of a vested interest, though they may deny it, in staying out of the spotlight, out of sight, preserving their linguistic freemasonry. This may have contributed to the ambivalence and imprecision of much of their public advocacy.

If a language is widely used, in widely diverse circumstances, it will grow and expand. Thus the relative invisibility of Esperanto has had little negative effect on its linguistic adequacy. Indeed, the fact that it has evolved from within, dominated by its most accomplished speakers, has meant that it has both preserved its unity and expanded its terminology and precision remarkably effectively. With over a century of literary tradition behind it, and with frequent use by various interest groups and professional organizations, it is no longer an experiment, but a language fully equipped for more general application.

Esperanto was seriously considered as a possible lingua franca for the League of Nations in the early 1920s (Lapenna, 1969a), though it has had less attention at the United Nations (Lapenna, 1969b and 1970–71, provide a history up to the 1960s). A petition presented to the United Nations in its early days calling for the use of Esperanto was sidetracked to UNESCO, where it was eventually transformed a dozen years later into a resolution merely noting the contribution of Esperanto to international understanding and noting the willingness of certain member-states to introduce it in their schools. UNESCO did not endorse Esperanto, nor did it commit its members to supporting it.

A later petition to the United Nations, presented in the 1960s, was again successfully deflected, this time by the Secretariat. Finally, in 1985, a UNESCO resolution called on member-states to encourage the study of Esperanto—the first time that an organ of the United Nations had done more than "note" its existence. But there is surely little disagreement that, for whatever reasons, efforts even to put Esperanto on the agenda of intergovernmental organizations have had little success.

If the 1985 UNESCO resolution, limited though it was, nevertheless went beyond that of 1954, this may be because there has recently been a shift in the line of argument used by advocates of Esperanto. New leadership and changed realities in the 1970s led to the inversion of the importance of the two arguments for Esperanto: the question of equality began to receive more play than the question of efficiency. Increasingly, Esperanto speakers were obliged to recognize that the United Nations did quite well in getting its business done. However, they also recognized that claims that the language regime was fair or egalitarian were palpably erroneous.

Latching on to the debate about communication rights and the free flow of information, Esperanto speakers argued that the domination of certain languages on the world scene perpetuated inequality and imbalance in the accessibility and flow of information. They maintained that this inequality was reinforced by the UN's language policies, and they pleaded for a different solution not because the present language regime did not work, but because its outcomes were unfair.

In so doing, they found a sympathetic audience among the least enfranchised nations, but their reasoning was in turn buried beneath the avalanche of opposition to such rallying-cries as the New World Information and Communication Order and the New International Economic Order. Their language merits reconsideration, linked now in a different way with the arguments about efficiency and cost. If the tacit acceptance of English as the lingua franca at the United Nations is dependent upon the maintenance of language services producing translations read by limited numbers of readers and interpretation listened to primarily by delegates checking to see if it is accurate, perhaps it is time to recognize that this is a very expensive means of maintaining communication and preserving the political status quo.

The advocates of Esperanto developed in the 1970s a new approach to the use of their language by the UN. Under the guidance of Australian Ambassador Ralph L. Harry, they suggested a program for its gradual introduction that might lead to radical realignment over time, but would in the short run produce relatively little disruption (see Piron and Tonkin, 1979, Harry and Mandel, 1979). This program posited a first stage in which Esperanto would be introduced as a language requiring only passive comprehension by the vast majority of users. The language would be introduced as one of those offered by the UN's language-teaching services, which would primarily stress reading and listening skills. Such skills are for the most part relatively easily acquired. Certain documents would be translated into Esperanto and made available to all member-states.

Later, once enough users had a passive, reading knowledge of the language, some of these documents would no longer be provided in six languages, but in Esperanto alone. A similar system would be applied to interpretation: gradual introduction in addition to the existing six languages, followed by gradual use as a language of interpretation instead of these languages. No one would be obliged to use Esperanto actively, i.e., to speak it or write it: it would be one of the languages of translation and interpretation, and ultimately, at least in some sectors, the only such language.

Perhaps, over time, active use of the language would follow. Perhaps also the United Nations would decide to augment the number of languages used and served in its formal business, since with only one language to work with in translation and interpretation, the language services would be freed up to take on new tasks. Thus a greater sense of equality would be introduced, and more languages, and hence more member-states, would be enfranchised. More delegates could use their own native languages in debate and written communication, where rhetorical skills are most important, and where linguistic disadvantage tends to be most keenly felt, but would rely on Esperanto to understand the contributions of others.

The balance of power established in the early days of the United Nations and reflected at least in the make-up of the Security Council and perhaps also in the system of working languages is today increasingly open to question as the world has changed and the victorious allies of World War II no longer exclusively dominate the international scene. This gives Esperanto a new opportunity. While it is unlikely that its advocates will singlehandedly overcome the interests vested in the status quo, Ambassador Harry's proposal might, with a little help from those who believe that the future of the United Nations depends on its adapting to new realities, find its way on to the United Nations agenda. Once there, it could receive the serious and objective attention it merits.

References

Harry, Ralph, and Mark Mandel. *Language Equality in International Cooperation.* Esperanto Documents 21. Rotterdam: Universal Esperanto Association, 1979.

Janton, Pierre. *Esperanto: Language, Literature, and Community*. Albany, New York: SUNY P, 1993.
Jastrab, Marie-Josée. "Organizational vs. Individual Bilingualism: The Case of the United Nations Secretariat." In Jane Edwards and Humphrey Tonkin, ed. *Language Behavior in International Organizations*. Report of the Second Annual Conference of the Center for Research and Documentation on World Language Problems. New York: The Center,1984. 5–58.
Lapenna, Ivo. "La situation juridique des 'langues officielles' avant la fondation des Nations Unies." *La Monda Lingvo-Problemo* 1(1969): 5–18. Cited as 1969a.
———. "La situation juridique des langues sous le régime des Nations Unies." *La Monda Lingvo-Problemo* 1(1969): 87–106. Cited as 1969b.
———. "The Common Language Question before International Organizations." *La Monda Lingvo-Problemo* 2(1970): 83–102, 3 (1971): 11–30.
Piron, Claude, and Humphrey Tonkin. *Translation in International Organizations*. Esperanto Documents 20. Rotterdam: Universal Esperanto Association, 1979.

About the Contributors

Margareta Bowen (Ph.D., University of Vienna) is Head of the Division of Interpretation and Translation in the School of Languages and Linguistics at Georgetown University. Before moving to Georgetown, she was chief interpreter of the United Nations Industrial Development Organization and has been translator and interpreter for the Austrian Ministry of the Interior. Co-editor of *The Jerome Quarterly*, she is also co-author of *Steps to Consecutive Interpretation* and was guest co-editor of *Interpreting Yesterday, Today and Tomorrow*, Volume 4 in the Scholarly Monograph Series produced by the American Translators Association. She continues to accept interpreting assignments in addition to her work at Georgetown University.

Karen Case is Assistant Professor of Educational Administration at the University of Hartford, where she teaches in the doctoral program in educational leadership. She received a B.A. in English and a Master of Arts in Teaching from the University of Iowa, where she was a member of the Iowa Writers' Workshop. She holds a doctorate from the University of Connecticut. Her areas of scholarship include school restructuring, teacher decision making, and student empowerment.

Françoise Cestac recently retired from the United Nations after serving in a succession of assignments, including Assistant Secretary General, Director of the Office of Conference Services, and Director of the Division of Translation. She has used her good offices to co-sponsor the series of conferences from which this set of publications derives.

Joshua A. Fishman is Distinguished University Research Professor of Social Sciences, Emeritus, at Yeshiva University and Visiting Professor of Linguistics and Education at Stanford University. Currently in press are his forthcoming *Post Imperial English, Language in the Big Apple*, and *The Beloved Language: The Content of Positive Ethnolinguistic Consciousness*.

Jean Gazarian, a graduate of the University of Paris, joined the United Nations Secretariat in 1946 as a translator. In 1986, after 17 years as Director of the Division of General Assembly Affairs in the Office of the Secretary-General, he was appointed secretary of a group of international experts to review the efficiency of the United Nations. Since 1987, he has been Senior Fellow at the United Nations Institute for Training and Research, in which capacity he conducts seminars for diplomats accredited to the UN. He is the author of "Language Problems in International Organizations," which appeared in Volume 2 of this series.

Ronald J. Glossop (Ph.D., Washington University) is Professor of Philosophical Studies and Coordinator of Peace Studies at Southern Illinois University at Edwardsville. He is the author of *Philosophy: An Introduction to Its Probelms and Vocabulary* (Dell, 1974); *Confronting War: An Examination of Humanity's Most Pressing Problem* (McFarland, 1983; 3rd ed., 1994); and *World Federation? A Critical Analysis of Federal World Government* (McFarland, 1993). Glossop serves as First Vice President of the national World Federalist Association as well as Chairman of the Greater St. Louis chapter of World Federalists. He is Vice President of the Internacia Ligo de Esperantistaj Instruistoj.

Kurt E. Müller is author of *Language Competence: Implications for National Security* (Praeger-CSIS, 1986) and editor of *Language as Barrier and Bridge* (University Press of America, 1992), Volume 2 in this series, *Languages in Elementary Schools* (American Forum, 1989) and *Children and Languages* (National Council on Foreign Language and International Studies, 1988), among other works. He received a B.A. in languages from the City College of New York, an M.M.A.S. (politico-military affairs) from the U.S. Army Command and General Staff College, and A.M., M.Phil., and Ph.D. from Rutgers University.

Stephen B. Pearl recently retired from his post as Chief of English Interpretation at the United Nations. He has been actively pursuing his interest in the teaching of conference interpretation, primarily in Europe. He is scheduled to conduct a course on interpretation between English and Russian, sponsored jointly by the School of Slavonic and East European Studies of London University and Communicaid International, and another on Russian-English and French-English interpretation, in conjunction with Kellogg College, Oxford University.

Timothy Reagan is Associate Professor of Bilingual and Foreign Language Education at the University of Connecticut. His research interests include language policy and language planning, educational linguistics, the education of cultural and linguistic minority groups, and sign language studies. He has published extensively on issues of education reform, teacher education, and applied linguistics. He contributed a chapter on the comparative analysis of sign languages to Volume 2 in this series.

Alexandre K. Titov has been Chief of the Russian Translation Service at the United Nations since 1986. From 1974 to 1983, he served with the Ministry for Foreign Affairs of the USSR, and holds the rank of Counsellor. He majored in German, English, and French studies at the Foreign Languages Institute in Moscow and pursued postgraduate studies in international economic relations and international organizations the the Diplomatic Academy of the USSR.

Humphrey Tonkin is President of the University of Hartford and chairs the board of the Center for Research and Documentation on World Language Problems. Formerly Professor of English at the University of Pennsylvania, his scholarly interests are sixteenth century English literature and the study of international language problems and language planning. He has published widely on language, literature, and international education.

Lynn Visson has been a Staff Interpreter at the United Nations since 1980. She received her M.A. from Columbia University and Ph.D. (Slavic Languages and Literature) from Harvard University, and she has taught at Columbia University and Bryn Mawr College. Author of several books, including a work on simultaneous interpretation from Russian into English, a study of the poet Sergei Esenin, and a Russian cookbook, she has edited and translated several books and authored numerous articles on Russian language, literature, and culture. Of Russian background, she travels frequently to Russia and has been involved in numerous cultural exchange programs.

Helene Zimmer-Loew is Executive Director of the American Association of Teachers of German. She has held leadership positions in several foreign language associations as well as serving on the Board of Directors of the American Forum for Global Education. Before assuming her position at the AATG, she was coordinator of the Resource Allocation Plan and on the staff of the New York State Education Department. She has taught German and Spanish. She holds degrees from Connecticut College, Middlebury College, St. John's University, and the State University of New York at Albany.